Andrew Bernstein is the founder of ActivInsight, a process that is rapidly changing the way individuals and organizations around the world understand stress and resilience. His clients include Johnson & Johnson, Coca-Cola, Merrill Lynch, 20th Century Fox, Goldman Sachs, ʳgan Stanley, Wachovia, Citigroup, Genentech, WPP, and Viacom. ɪs on the faculty at the Wharton School in the Executive Education vision, and also teaches pro bono at not-for-profit organizations like hoenix House and City Year. His website is mythofstress.com.

Praise for Andrew Bernstein and
The Myth of Stress:

'Look out Anthony Robbins, move over Deepak Chopra, there's a quiet storm moving up through this state and beyond. His name is Andrew Bernstein ... He's an intelligent, calm and soft-spoken person who uses reason and logic to quiet the mind'

Vision magazine

'Bernstein's volume is an outstanding guide to understanding the nature of stress and how to handle it. The book provides numerous insights and techniques for anyone experiencing stress – and who doesn't?'

Aaron T. Beck, MD, founder of Cognitive Therapy

'*The Myth of Stress* is a compelling, compassionate book about our suffering when we fight reality and the transformation that is possible when we don't. I loved it'

Geneen Roth, author of *When Food Is Love* and *Women, Food, and God*

'Andrew Bernstein has brought some much-needed common sense to the subject of stress and that alone makes this book a winner'

Caroline Myss, author of *Defy Gravity* and *Invisible Acts of Power*

'Bernstein has created a wonderful, accessible how-to manual for regular people wanting to feel better. This WORKS!'

Kathleen DesMaisons, PhD, author of *Potatoes Not Prozac*

ANDREW BERNSTEIN

The Myth of Stress

Where Stress *Really* Comes From and How to Live a Happier, Healthier Life

PIATKUS

First published in the US in 2010 by Free Press, a division of Simon & Schuster, Inc.
First published in Great Britain in 2010 by Piatkus

A CIP catalogue record for this book
is available from the British Library.

ISBN 978-0-7499-4299-1

Printed and bound in Great Britain by
MPG Books, Bodmin, Cornwall.

Papers used by Piatkus are natural, renewable and
recyclable products sourced from well-managed forests and certified
in accordance with the rules of the Forest Stewardship Council.

Mixed Sources
Product group from well-managed
forests and other controlled sources
www.fsc.org Cert no. SGS-COC-004081
© 1996 Forest Stewardship Council
FSC

Piatkus
An imprint of
Little, Brown Book Group
100 Victoria Embankment
London EC4Y 0DY

An Hachette UK Company
www.hachette.co.uk

www.piatkus.co.uk

CONTENTS

CONTENTS

Part Two:
INSIGHT IN ACTION

CONTENTS

CONTENTS

PREFACE

How I Came to Write This Book

What is stress? Where does it come from? And is it possible to live without it?

I began asking these questions twenty-five years ago under some challenging personal circumstances. When I was fourteen, my father passed away unexpectedly. Two years later my little half sister was killed in a car accident, and a year after that, two more friends of mine died. While my high school classmates worried about SAT scores, I wondered if I would ever be happy again. At one of the wake services an older gentleman approached me to see if I had any questions he could answer. I did: how long would the pain last? He looked down at me soberly for a moment and said, "The rest of your life."

I seriously hope this man was not a therapist.

Looking back at that answer now, I'm grateful for two reasons. First, I'm grateful because his response was so absurdly bleak that it started me on a quest to find a better one. And second, I'm grateful because that answer wasn't true, though it was years before I understood why.

After high school I attended Johns Hopkins University, dreaming of becoming a surgeon, but in my sophomore year the English department seduced me. I had thought English majors lounged around in black turtlenecks arguing about semicolons. In fact, they are taught to think critically about life, using literature as a mirror to see the world. Whether or not that would make me employable, I liked the idea of learning to think critically about things. I enjoyed it and did well, even beginning a PhD in literature after college. And then my girlfriend broke up with me, and I wanted answers to my big questions again. So I dropped out of graduate school, moved to an island in Maine, got a dog, and began working in a bakery. When overwhelmed, some people go postal. I went Thoreau.

When I wasn't delivering bread or hiking the Maine woods with my dog, I was reading, but this time instead of literature I read self-help. Traditional, alternative, Eastern, Western, ancient, contemporary—I read widely and found that my years of academic training had taught me to quickly identify an author's underlying argument and test its validity. Now, instead of applying this X-ray vision to literary criticism, I applied it to the world of personal transformation. What was the author really saying? Did his or her process actually work? If so, how?

I spent the rest of my twenties living in different cities, working as a freelance writer and continuing my education in self-transformation. Somewhat randomly, I sold a screenplay to the Muppets (yes, the Muppets) and moved to Los Angeles. I had dabbled on and off in comedy writing, and several agents had encouraged me to consider it as a career. And it was there in Los Angeles, after a few years of swinging through the jungles of Hollywood as a screenwriter, that I met someone who changed my life.

Let me say here that those three words—*changed my life*—always raise a big red flag for me. Anybody selling anything claims it will change your life—a weight-loss program, a skin-care product, a vegetable peeler. In a way, these claims are true. Yesterday I had no vegetable peeler. Today I have one, so my life *has* literally changed, and just look at these carrots! But when we reflect back on the things that have really changed our lives, I suspect we will not find them in our kitchen drawers. In my case, I met a woman who helped me understand how stress was created and how I could take it apart.

That woman's name was Byron Katie. A silver-haired grandmother with sparkling blue eyes, Katie, as everyone calls her, is the founder of a transformational process called The Work. The Work is a sequence of four provocative and penetrating questions that can change how you see any difficult situation. I found it to be both simple and surprisingly effective, and I found Katie herself to be unshakably peaceful and loving, with a great sense of humor. After spending several months getting to know her and her process better, I gave up screenwriting and became the creative director of her company, in charge of advertising, marketing, and design.

Over the next three years, I did The Work a lot. The clearer I got on specific challenges, the more easily I could see how stress and conflict in general were created. Part of my job was making this information available to others. The Work already had thousands of fans around the world, and today, with Katie's bestselling books, it may be millions. But some people, for whatever reason, found the process difficult to grasp. At first I thought this was a shortcoming of my marketing efforts, but eventually I realized that people simply respond differently to different things. And that got me thinking.

When it comes to getting in better physical shape, we have plenty of choices: walking, running, spinning, yoga, swimming, Pilates, CrossFit. There is no shortage of options, with new ones gaining popularity every year. But when it comes to getting in better *mental* shape and resolving the problems in our lives, far fewer choices come to mind, and these tend to fall short of full mainstream acceptance. Why is that?

It's certainly not because of a lack of need. How many people do you know who struggle with stress on a daily basis, or who have complained of some hardship for months or even years? Yet many of us view the available options as either too clinical ("I'm not doing that"), or too touchy-feely ("I'm not doing that either"), and as a result we don't do anything. It isn't that the existing solutions don't work. Processes like The Work and Cognitive Therapy, to name two of my favorites, have helped many, many people. But the shoe has to fit the foot, not the other way around, and it seemed to me that millions of us were walking around skeptical, barefoot, and in pain.

So, I wondered, what about designing a new shoe? What if the dynamics of personal transformation could be taught in a mainstream way appealing to those who just wanted to live with less stress, without any clinical or spiritual overtones? I started to envision a new process, and I left Katie's company to explore that vision. I still highly recommend that you learn more about The Work at thework.com. It's a very powerful process, and I owe it and Katie an inestimable debt of gratitude.

After spending several months revisiting the techniques I had explored earlier and studying many I hadn't, I developed a process I first called Mental Yoga, a sequence of cognitive steps that would "stretch" your mind out of stress the way yoga stretches your body. I shared it first with family and friends, and then, in the summer of 2004, I began offering public workshops.

Word spread surprisingly fast. A participant at one of my first workshops took me aside to say that this technique had helped her enormously with a long-standing relationship issue, and that she happened to be writing a piece on transformation for a bestselling magazine. Would it be all right if she featured me? (Okay, twist my arm.) Others asked if I could help colleagues at their companies, but . . . what about calling it something else? The name Mental Yoga was a little confusing—some people brought yoga mats or expected meditation—so I changed it to ActivInsight. Insight is the heart of transformation, and this process makes it an active experience.

As you'll see in the chapters that follow, stress always indicates a lack of insight, and the seven steps of ActivInsight remedy this. They help you gently but directly challenge the way you understand your situation, provoking a profound shift in perspective in just a matter of minutes. The more you do it, the more insights you have—into relationships, money, success, body image, interpersonal conflict, or anything else—and the less you experience stress. It's not that you become better able to "handle" stress. The stress is actually no longer produced.

I've now taught ActivInsight to people from more than fifteen countries, including thousands of leaders at Fortune 500 companies. Because there's no jargon and nothing touchy-feely about it—and because it helps people stay focused no matter what is happening— CEOs and senior management teams have embraced it. I teach regularly at the University of Pennsylvania's Wharton School in the Executive Education division, where my Resilience 101 program is featured as part of leadership training. And I teach pro bono at some of the country's most respected not-for-profit organizations, helping participants use ActivInsight to deal with many of life's biggest challenges.

I've learned from all these workshops that stress always works the same way. The issues that we each face may differ, but the basic dynamics of stress do not. Yet these dynamics are widely misunderstood by stress researchers, and have been for more than half a century. As a result, most people today are confused about where stress actually comes from, which leads to disastrous effects on our health, our happiness, and our ability to handle changes smoothly and get things done.

This book is intended to help fix that. This is the book that my workshop participants have been asking me to write so they could share ActivInsight with their families and friends. And, on a more personal note, it's the book I would have wanted to read when I began seeking answers long ago. Part 1 teaches you what really causes stress and how ActivInsight works. Part 2 guides you step-by-step as you apply ActivInsight to more than a dozen challenging situations. Together, these give you a complete reeducation in the nature of stress and a simple tool you can use to regain peace of mind anytime you need to for the rest of your life.

So where does stress really come from, and how can you live without it? Let's get started and I'll show you.

PART ONE

THE TRUTH ABOUT STRESS

CHAPTER 1

The Myth Exposed

Where does stress come from? Here's what most people think: stress comes from the enormous pressure and responsibilities in your life. It comes from your deadlines and ambitions. It comes from a loss of control, or from having insufficient resources, such as time and money. It comes from the state of your romantic life (or lack thereof). It comes from the economy, the environment, and the unprecedented changes taking place around the world. It comes from your mother-in-law. That one may be worth repeating twice. It comes from your mother-in-law.

In short, stress comes from all the things in your life that aren't going quite as smoothly as you would like. For most people, that's a pretty long list. Some of these things you can change, of course, and you do. But some resist your best efforts, and so you experience stress. Since everyone around you seems to be in the same boat, you resign yourself to the fact that life is inherently stressful. "That's life," you say with a sigh. You just have to accept it.

Actually, that's not life. The belief that life is stressful is part of a myth, a misunderstanding based on a faulty interpretation of the nature of stress. And, just to put a few more cards on the table, you do not have a stressful job (no matter what your job may be), you are under no pressure at school, at work, or at home, and your mother-in-law (or whoever else seems to drive you crazy) is not a stressor. In fact, there is no such thing as a stressor. This is yet another part of the myth of stress.

Let me make clear that I'm *not* saying that stress itself is a myth. Stress is very real, and if you're reading these words, it's a safe bet that you're living with more than your fair share of it. The myth involves *where stress comes from* and *what you can do about it.* The stress in your life didn't get there the way you think it did, and it's not going to go away unless you learn where it really came from and how to address it more effectively. That's what this book is going to teach you. In this chapter, we'll take a closer look at where stress research unwittingly went astray decades ago, creating the myth that almost everyone believes today.

So let's begin at the beginning by asking, what is stress exactly? According to the *American Heritage Dictionary,* stress is defined as follows.

STRESS: A mentally or emotionally disruptive or upsetting condition occurring in response to adverse external influences and capable of affecting physical health, usually characterized by increased heart rate, a rise in blood pressure, muscular tension, irritability, and depression.

That probably seems pretty accurate to you. After all, it's in the dictionary for a reason—smart people have written this definition to line up with common experience. Nevertheless, it's wrong. Look at it again. Can you see where it's wrong?

The first part, I admit, is true. Stress *is* a mentally or emotionally disruptive or upsetting condition. Stress is not just anxiety about getting things done. I'll use the term "stress" in this book to include anger, frustration, jealousy, heartache, sadness, fear, worry, resentment, regret, shame, and any other negative emotion you experience, large or small. Anything you are bothered by—anything that you think about with even the slightest degree of annoyance—qualifies as stress, and I'm going to teach you how to eliminate it. But as far as the dictionary goes, that first part of the definition passes muster.

The latter part of the definition is also true. Without a doubt, stress can affect your physical health. The Centers for Disease Control estimate that 75 to 90 percent of medical visits are stress related, and the list of conditions caused or exacerbated by stress is growing fast. It already includes the six leading causes of death. If you want to improve your health, you want to lessen the amount of stress in your life.

But what about that middle part, the part about stress "occurring in response to adverse external influences"? A quick mental scan of your life would seem to confirm this, as you imagine your responsibilities, your bills, that one special person who always gets under your skin. Those do seem to be "adverse external influences." Let's run with this for a moment and say that this, too, is correct. Why would people experience stress in response to "adverse external influences"? In the big picture of life on Earth, how would this response to "adverse external influences" have been helpful?

When asked this question, most people envision a time long ago when life on Earth looked dramatically different. There were no deadlines and traffic jams, and there was no pressure to perform well. There were, however, challenges. Big challenges. Big challenges with teeth, like the saber-toothed tiger. In fact, if you pick up almost any book on stress, you're practically guaranteed to read about the saber-toothed tiger and the role it played in the stress response. The story goes something like this . . .

Once upon a time, our caveman and cavewoman ancestors went foraging only to come across—a saber-toothed tiger. Our ancestors immediately experienced a surge of adrenaline, giving them extra energy to fight or run away. As you may remember from high school biology, this is called the fight-or-flight response. Those who had a strong fight-or-flight response were more likely to survive these encounters and would pass this response on to their offspring. Those who didn't have a strong fight-or-flight response, for obvious reasons, wouldn't. As a result, over millions of years, this hormonal surge was strengthened and became hardwired into us as an automatic response to (pay attention here) adverse external influences. And then something unusual happened.

In just a few thousand years—the mere blink of an eye from an evolutionary perspective—life changed radically. Civilizations were born. Cities emerged. And now, instead of facing the occasional saber-toothed tiger and the rare but helpful surge of hormones that accompanied it, we find ourselves surrounded by challenges on a daily basis: traffic jams, project deadlines, quarterly numbers, work/life balance, relationship crises, exams, child care, elder care, family conflicts, divorce, disease, economic downturns, geopolitical unrest, war, and so much more. As a result, our fight-or-flight response is going haywire. The number of "adverse external influences" has multiplied exponentially, so that some of us are living in a near-constant state of stress. It's as if saber-toothed tigers are everywhere, continually tripping our internal alarms. We've become victims of our own biology.

This story gets repeated in hundreds of contemporary articles and books written about stress. But where are the writers getting it from? It turns out they're getting this mostly from one man—the man who gave birth to the modern myth of stress and unintentionally got us all thinking about stress in exactly the wrong way. That man, the so-called father of stress, was Dr. Hans Selye. To break through the myth, we need to understand a little bit about who Selye was and what he accomplished.

In 1936, freshly out of medical school, Hans Selye began his career as a researcher at McGill University in Montreal. This was the golden age of endocrinology, when the discovery of new hormones splashed across the front pages of newspapers around the world and the scientists behind those discoveries won Nobel Prizes. Selye's lab was trying to isolate new sex hormones, and Selye, dreaming of making a breakthrough of his own, would go to the slaughterhouse each morning, bring a large bucket of fresh cow ovaries back to the lab, grind and mix them with formaldehyde as a preservative, and inject them into rats. If the rats exhibited symptoms that had never before been noted, it was likely the injection contained an undiscovered hormone that could be purified and used to help millions of people.

Lab work like this typically involves months of dead ends, but on one of his very first experiments, Selye hit the jackpot. After injecting rats with his ovarian extract mixture, Selye sacrificed them and noticed that all the rats exhibited the following three symptoms:

1. The adrenal glands (small structures perched on top of each kidney) were enlarged.
2. The thymuses, spleens, and lymph nodes (all parts of the immune system) had shrunk considerably.
3. There were deep bleeding ulcers in the stomach and intestines.

Selye reviewed the literature on ovarian extracts and found no mention of this triple response, or "triad." Eureka! Only twenty-eight years old and he was already on the verge of discovering a new ovarian hormone. He was ecstatic.

Selye's ecstasy diminished only slightly when he was able to produce the same triad with extracts from cow placentas. Perhaps, he reasoned, this new hormone was found both in ovaries *and* placentas. Hormones, after all, could be produced by more than one organ. Then he tested pituitary extracts and found the triad yet again. Over the next few weeks, Selye tested extracts from kidneys, livers, spleens—all resulting in the same triad being formed. How was this possible? Was this a general hormone found in any organ of the body? Selye had never heard of such a thing. He also wondered why the least pure extracts—the ones containing the most preservative—caused the most pronounced symptoms.

And then it hit him. With great reluctance, Selye picked up a bottle of formaldehyde from the counter and injected some directly into a rat. Forty-eight hours later, looking at the sacrificed rat's organs, Selye couldn't believe his eyes. The triad was the strongest yet. He hadn't discovered a hormone at all. He was merely seeing the harmful internal effects of being injected with a toxic preservative.

Selye was crushed. For days he couldn't work. Here he had thought he was making the enormous discovery of a new hormonal response, and it was just the body's reaction to toxic exposure. He had wasted time and resources (as well as the lives of the rats), and was embarrassed and ashamed.

But then he had another thought. What if instead of discovering a *specific* hormonal reaction, he had discovered a *general* one triggered by any big challenge? To test this, Selye exposed rats to other challenges, such as intense exercise, vibration, noise, starvation, heat, and cold. When dozens of different circumstances produced the exact same internal triad of symptoms, Selye reflected on what he was seeing and came up with a novel theory: the rats were physically reacting to being pushed beyond their ability to adapt to challenging circumstances. Selye first called this the General Adaptation Syndrome, and then, more simply, the stress syndrome. In a word, Hans Selye had discovered stress.

Obviously, stress itself had existed long before this, but it had never before been placed successfully in a medical context. In fact, only a few years earlier, Selye's idol, the great physiologist Walter Cannon, had strongly recommended that the medical community pay more attention to stress, and his plea fell on deaf ears. But timing is everything, and as World War II unfolded, the medical and public interest in stress mushroomed. Military leaders wanted to know how to train more resilient soldiers and how to treat those who were returning from battle emotionally damaged. Laypeople anxious about the war wanted to live with less worry and fear. As a result, articles and books on stress became a part of the public discourse for the first time. And with his discovery of this internal adaptive triad, Hans Selye recognized that he could leap to the forefront of this newly created field and make a name for himself.

And that's exactly what he did. Over the next four decades, Selye wrote more than thirty books on the subject of stress, with titles like *The Stress of Life, Stress Without Distress,* and *Stress in Health and Disease.* He published approximately 1,700 papers addressing stress and psychiatry, stress and aging, stress and cancer, stress and disease. He created the world's largest stress library—indexing 110,000 articles in more than twenty languages—intending that all stress research globally be coordinated through his Canadian office. He lectured constantly, appeared frequently in the pages of *Time* magazine as the founder of the stress concept, and even published a code of human behavior that he felt people and nations should adopt based on his stress research. Selye believed that he had discovered one of nature's great physical laws, and he wanted everyone to know about it.

In all these efforts, what exactly was Selye saying? Ultimately, Hans Selye defined stress as "the nonspecific response of the body to any demand placed upon it." The heart of his theory was this concept of nonspecificity. Here's the basic gist: If you sit in a sauna, you sweat. If you sit in cold water, you shiver. Sweating and shivering are *specific* responses because they involve pathways unique to those conditions. But Selye argued that beneath these specific reactions was a *non*specific physiological response, an internal reaction that took place across the board whenever a living creature faced a taxing demand. Whether it was challenges at work, difficulties with a relationship, concerns about money, or exposure to physical stimuli like heat, cold, or drugs, these all triggered the same triad indicative of poor adaptation. *That,* according to Selye, was stress.

Since stress is a physical reaction to any great change, Selye explained, it's inevitable in life. After all, there is always some change the body has to adapt to (food, temperature, fatigue, etc.). The best we can do is accept it and try to cope using techniques such as relaxation. Most of us still believe this today, even if we've never heard the name Hans Selye.

Throughout the 1950s and '60s, Selye's theory was tacitly accepted as true, and it gave birth to the modern "stress management" movement based on relaxation and similar techniques. Even the skeptics agreed that this adaptation theory and Selye's efforts to communicate it had helped generate immense interest both in public and professional circles. This is an enormous accomplishment. Selye's pioneering research into the hormones released during stress is also an important body of work that laid the foundation for much of our current knowledge.

But let's step back a moment to consider the big picture of what Hans Selye claimed to have discovered. Based on the reactions of his rats to a wide variety of different conditions, Selye proposed that stress is the nonspecific response of the body to any demand. Is that actually what his experiments revealed?

In the mid-1970s, another research scientist suggested that Hans Selye had made a crucial mistake. To demonstrate this, Dr. John W. Mason of the Walter Reed Army Institute of Research ingeniously modified Selye's experiments. For example, instead of submitting animals to a blast of heat as Selye had, Mason raised the temperature slowly, little by little. If heat was, in fact, a stressor, the final hot temperature should still trigger the stress response. Selye had also deprived some rats of food at mealtime, saying that nutritional deprivation was a stressor. Mason wondered, what if the deprived animals were given nonnutritive food pellets instead, so that they felt included at mealtime but were still nutritionally starved? Would it produce the same physiological stress reaction? And what if, instead of being forced to exercise as Selye's rats had been, subjects exercised hard but without compulsion? Would stress still result?

Mason had an important advantage in his experiments. In the 1930s and '40s, Selye had to sacrifice rats and study their organs visually to see the effects of stress. But technology had improved by Mason's day so that he could draw blood and very precisely measure stress hormones in living subjects. Doing this, Mason found that, if you controlled for psychological reactions, there was little or no stress response. When the heat was raised gradually, when the test subjects could munch on pellets that had zero nutritional content, or when they exercised hard but were comfortable, there was no rise in hormone production. In other words, Selye's rats weren't stressed out because they were reacting "nonspecifically" to heat, cold, vibration, starvation, noise, and countless other conditions. They were stressed out *because they were upset.*

Mason wrote a series of brilliant articles challenging Selye's theory point by point, explaining exactly why a *physiological* theory of stress didn't work and a *psychological* theory did. But Selye refused to admit defeat, maintaining to his death in 1982 that stress was physically triggered. Selye had the "first mover" advantage, having spread his message all over the world for decades. It became part of the story of stress, or what I call the myth, incorporated into thousands of books globally with their tales of fight-or-flight responses and saber-toothed tigers. Like Earth seeming flat, this myth appeared to be true. It was what you could call sticky. And for most people, it still sticks. We continue to believe that stress is a physical and emotional reaction to adverse external influences, that it comes from deadlines or breakups or health challenges, and we talk about how stressful our lives are, and how people and things stress us out. But just as the Earth is not flat, this myth about stress is simply not true.

The truth is that stress is not a physical process with a psychological component, as Selye proclaimed, but a *psychological* process with a physical component. Put another way, stress doesn't come from what's going on in your life—it comes from *your thoughts about* what's going on in your life. Your job isn't stressful—*your thoughts about* your job are stressful. Your relationship doesn't stress you out—*your thoughts about* your relationship stress you out. All stress is an inside job, a result of subconscious assumptions.

Think about this for a few moments and you may realize what this means: in reality, *there is no such thing as a stressor.* Nothing has the inherent power to *cause* stress in you. Things happen (divorce, layoffs, disease, etc.), and you experience stress—or you don't—depending on what you *think* about those things. Stress is a function of beliefs, not circumstances.

The same is true for pressure. When I first started teaching ActivInsight at large organizations, I met with a very smart senior executive who was proud that his company didn't use the confusing word *stress*. Instead, he explained, they used the word *pressure*. Unfortunately, this is still part of the myth. Unless you're a commercial scuba diver, you don't work under pressure. Stress and pressure are reflections of your mental landscape, of the beliefs and assumptions you hold about the world. If you feel pressure, it's because of something you're thinking. It comes from the inside out, not the outside in.

And this is how it's always been. Ten thousand years ago, saber-toothed tigers didn't trigger a fight-or-flight response in our ancestors. It was *thoughts about tigers* that triggered this response. If a caveman and cavewoman were sitting in their cave and a saber-toothed tiger sneaked up on them—and they had no idea that it was there—those cavepeople would not have experienced stress. Yes, they might have died, but don't let that distract you from the point here.

Until there's a thought, there's no stress. And if the cavewoman *thought* she saw a tiger but it was actually a bunch of reeds, she *would* have experienced stress even though there was no tiger, because stress is a psychological process. It may not be a fully conscious experience—in many cases these responses begin in the oldest parts of the brain before conscious awareness gets involved—but it is still a mental process of interpretation. Stress never comes directly from your circumstances. It comes from your thoughts about your circumstances. This is the Iron Rule of Stress. There are no exceptions to this rule.

A half century of stress dogma doesn't go down without a fight, and most people at this point have a number of questions. For example, what about physical stress, such as when you work long hours or don't get enough sleep? Is that also based on your thought process?

In a word, no. That kind of stress—the wear and tear on your body as it adapts to different physical conditions like exercise and changes in temperature—*is* inevitable in life, and if that were all Hans Selye was talking about, I would agree with him completely. There is no way to avoid physiological adaptation to changing conditions. But when most of us say we're stressed-out, we don't mean that our bodies are having a hard time thermoregulating. We mean that we're emotionally overwhelmed. Selye collapsed this distinction, mixing physical stress and psychological stress together into a single stress concept. Some of the same internal reactions may take place during each process, but they're initiated in very different ways. You can be asleep or even comatose and undergo physical stress as your cells continue reacting to change, whereas psychological stress requires the participation of thought.

To make things clearer, I would refer to the body's adaptive reactions to temperature, fatigue, lack of nutrition, and other biological challenges as homeostasis. *Homeostasis,* you may remember, is the word Walter Cannon coined to describe the body's ability to maintain a steady state in spite of fluctuating conditions. When it's hot outside, you maintain homeostasis by sweating, for example. Instead of calling heat a stressor, as Selye did, I would classify it as a homeostatic challenge, and I would reserve the word *stress* for the psychologically produced emotional responses that most of us care about. Of course, these processes are interrelated, and you can stress yourself out thinking about your body's ability to balance itself (such as when you're sick). But recognizing that they're not the same process will help you approach both the body and the mind more effectively.

Another question that often comes up is, isn't some stress good for us? This is also part of the myth and has an interesting history. Because Selye wanted people to see stress as the body's nonspecific reaction to *any* demand, he had unwittingly painted himself into a corner: What about the physical demands that result from things we enjoy, like sports or sex? Were these also stressful? Realizing that he had to include these as well, Selye coined a new word: *eustress.* So there was *distress* for things that were stressful and negative, and *eustress* for things that were stressful and positive. Selye suggested that people minimize the distress and maximize the eustress in their lives.

This makes sense only if you see stress as biological. But when you recognize that stress is psychological in origin, the idea of eustress falls apart—these would just be homeostatic challenges that we enjoy. The concept of "good stress" also makes no sense in practical terms. Have you ever heard anyone say, "I had great sex last night! Wow, it was stressful"? As far as ActivInsight is concerned, there is no such thing as "good stress." There may be physical challenges that you enjoy, but no one enjoys stress. The fewer negative emotions you live with, the better you feel.

As another offshoot of the myth of stress, many people believe that stress is a motivator. Here we need to distinguish between stress and stimulation. Being stimulated is good. Having goals and deadlines and staying engaged is important. Peak performance happens when you are fully engaged and in flow. But this is not stressful. Athletes call this "the zone," and it feels magical because there is great activity with no stress at all. Stress, on the other hand, whether it's anxiety, frustration, anger, or other negative emotions, limits your ability to perform in a number of ways. It makes you less creative, it reduces your ability to concentrate, it makes effective communication harder, and it shortens the amount of time you can sustain an effort. The bottom line is, stress is a demotivator. If you're stressed out and still succeeding, you're succeeding in spite of your stress, not because of it.

Another question that often arises is, if stress comes from your thoughts and not your circumstances, does that mean it's all in your head? Stress may start in your head, but the effects on your body, your feelings, and your behaviors are very real. Look at all the things that people do as a result of the negative emotions in their lives, from eating junk food, to smoking and drinking, to fighting with others, even waging war. These behaviors stem from something taking place in your thought process, but they have tangible and dramatic effects on the world around you. Recognizing that stress begins in your head instead of in your surroundings does not in any way diminish the reality of the experience. It simply enables you to address it more strategically at its source.

So what about vacations, exercise, yoga, relaxation, and massage, or anti-anxiety medications, or, for that matter, drinking and drugs? Don't these also eliminate stress? These solutions relieve the *effects* that stress produces in your body, but they don't address the *cause*, so the stress tends to return. Have you noticed that, a few hours after your workout, or a few days after your vacation, the same old issues slowly reemerge? The key to *eliminating* stress, and not just managing or escaping it, is to create a fundamental and lasting shift in the way you actually think.

How? That's what ActivInsight was designed for. Once you learn how to generate an insight into the things that trouble you, you can apply it to anything. It's as if you're going to the source of stress in your mind and flipping a switch from on to off, so the stress no longer gets produced, even though the external circumstances may appear exactly the same. That's the power of insight. In the next chapter, I'll show you how it works.

CHAPTER 2

The Power
of Insight

At the beginning of the great Russian novel *Anna Karenina,* Leo Tolstoy suggested that happy families are all alike, but every unhappy family is unhappy in its own way. From a dramatic point of view, Tolstoy was right—every story of unhappiness is a little different, and Anna's unhappy story is one of the best ever written. But from the point of view of how stress works, Tolstoy was grossly mistaken. The truth is that every individual and family is unhappy *in exactly the same way*—as a by-product of a certain kind of thinking. Anna Karenina was not struck by unhappiness in the same way one is struck by lightning. Unhappiness arises internally, through the subconscious mind. And it is dissolved through insight.

Insight is a built-in, though generally overlooked, feature of your brain's operating system. You've already had insights that resulted in less stress in your life. You just may not have realized what was taking place. For example, have you ever been angry at someone for something he said or did and then later discovered that you had misunderstood the situation and that he didn't actually say or do quite what you had thought? During that experience, you didn't try to change how you felt, nor did you "let go" of your previous belief. You simply realized that you were mistaken, and that realization instantly and automatically shifted both how you felt and how you acted. That's the power of insight.

The word *insight* is generally defined as the "penetrating act of seeing into something more clearly." For our purposes, I define *insight* more specifically as *the realization that what you had believed to be true is actually false so that the real truth emerges.* In the example above concerning a friend, you believed that something had taken place, and that belief was proven false by new information. As the false belief falls away, the truth that you hadn't been able to see is revealed. This kind of insight has the power to dissolve even the biggest issues because it completely shifts your perspective on a situation. But in the tool kit of personal transformation, insight tends to get overlooked.

The main reason we overlook it is because insight usually happens passively instead of actively. As a result, a shift in perspective can seem to take place on its own as a function of time. Have you heard the expression "Time heals all wounds"? That may be true for most physical wounds, but it's not true when it comes to psychological ones. I'm sure you know someone who has stubbornly carried a grudge for years, and you can probably think of issues in your own life that have lingered on despite time's passing.

As enough time passes, however, we tend to stumble across new information that changes our point of view. So it's actually insight that heals us, not time. The problem is that this insight can be a long time coming, so we end up spending days, weeks, months, or even years stuck in the same psychological emotional groove.

ActivInsight distills the dynamics of insight into a simple process you can use to consciously provoke a shift in your thinking anytime you feel angry, upset, or stressed out. It makes insight active (hence the name) and available on demand. As with any skill, it takes some practice and guidance. I often compare this to skiing.

You don't start out skiing the advanced black diamond runs. You start by watching someone else ski, which you're going to do in this chapter, and then you hit the bunny slopes and try it for yourself, which you'll do in part 2. As the book proceeds, the challenges will get more intense and you'll progress from skiing beginner runs to intermediates. Eventually, before this book ends, you and I are going to tackle an advanced black diamond run together.

In the preface, I mentioned that I teach ActivInsight at several not-for-profit organizations. One of these is Phoenix House, the largest residential addiction recovery program in the United States. Residents are often mandated by a judge to live at Phoenix House for a certain length of time instead of, or in addition to, serving a prison sentence. Theoretically, they use this time to develop discipline, go on job interviews, and rehabilitate themselves. In reality, many of them remain angry at the system and just want to finish their stay and get out, returning to the same thoughts, feelings, and behaviors (including drug use) they had when they entered the program.

When I created ActivInsight, I wanted to test it not just with people who were eagerly seeking personal transformation, but also with those who were somewhat resistant to it. Recovering addicts just out of prison seemed an interesting population to explore, so I approached the Phoenix House near where I lived in Los Angeles and demonstrated the process to the staff psychologist and the program director. Both liked what they saw and agreed to put together a small group of men to meet with me once a week for six weeks as a pilot. I was told that one man in particular, whom I'll call Dudley, was a bit of a problem, picking fights with other residents and generally disrupting the house. Apparently, he was going to give me the test I was looking for.

Five men and I met around a table in a small third-floor classroom overlooking the Pacific Ocean: Jeff, who was white, in his twenties, and looked like some of the clean-cut kids I grew up with in Manhattan. Dave, a Vietnam vet with sandy gray hair and no front teeth. Manny, a smiling Mexican "tweaker"—he had been addicted to methamphetamine. Elwood, a young, skinny, black man with a quick wit. And Dudley, who was six foot three, in his late forties, and walked with a slight limp. Dudley could have come from Central Casting for the stereotypical "big black man" in white directors' prison movies. He slid down in his chair and stared at the table. Even when Dudley was silent, though, it was clear that the rest of the room was listening to him.

I introduced myself and told them a little bit about what I was doing there. Then I handed out blank sheets of paper and asked them to write down what was stressful in their lives. This is how you start ActivInsight, by translating your stressful thoughts onto paper. I asked them to write short, simple sentences, ideally using the words *should* or *shouldn't*. After a few minutes we went around the room and they each shared one or two statements from their paper: "My family should be less critical." "People shouldn't be so negative." "I should have more money." Then we got to Dudley. He sounded tired and bitter. "I shouldn't be here," he said.

At first I thought he meant in the classroom, but he corrected me. "I shouldn't be here at Phoenix House," Dudley said. "I should be home."

The rest of the guys responded immediately. "Yeah, me too." "I shouldn't be here, either." "That's how I feel." It was unanimous. I've since worked with residents at other Phoenix House locations, and that belief—"I shouldn't be here"—is incredibly common. It's also incredibly problematic, because instead of trying to learn new skills or prepare for their release, residents stew in their resentment and fight the system. The same is true in prisons and rehab clinics around the world, which ostensibly exist to foster transformation, but in reality are often stagnant pools of resistance and proclaimed victimhood. The statement "I shouldn't be here" lies at the heart of it. So that's the first topic we chose, transferring it to the ActivInsight worksheet.

You always use a worksheet when doing ActivInsight because it helps you have a much deeper insight than if you tried to do this in your head, and it gives you something you can review later. There's a worksheet included at the back of this book for you to photocopy, or you can download and print worksheets from mythofstress.com.

Look at your worksheet and you'll see that it's just seven steps. In Step 1, you write down the statement you're working on, phrasing it in a way that's concise and honest, and, most of the time, using the words *should* or *shouldn't*. It's important to be concise. You don't want to write something such as, "Tom should have listened to me when I told him what to do because I knew this would happen, that idiot." Just "Tom should have listened to me" is fine. Similarly, if you're stressed out by thoughts about your mother, you wouldn't write: "I don't understand why my mother is so selfish. I do everything for her. Shouldn't she appreciate me more?" Distill it to one statement (not a question) and use *should* or *shouldn't* in this way: "My mother shouldn't be so selfish" or "My mother should be more grateful for what I do" or "My mother should appreciate me more." You can do multiple worksheets with different phrasings and have slightly different insights. You can even write statements that don't use *should* or *shouldn't*—I'll give some examples of these later—but the should/shouldn't formulation is the easiest to start with, and in most cases the best at capturing your emotional charge, even when you're a pro.

Beginners often think that they're going to need hundreds of worksheets to work through their issues, but in my experience most people are troubled by the same handful of beliefs over and over. It really doesn't take that many worksheets to see a big difference in your life. The first few require some guidance, though, so the men at Phoenix House and I all wrote the following together:

1 Write a concise, complete sentence describing something that you experience as stressful. It's helpful to use the words "should" or "shouldn't." (Ex.: "They should listen to me.")

> *I shouldn't be here.*

_____

_____

That's it for Step 1.

In Step 2, you rate how strongly you believe this statement on a scale from 0 to 10, 10 being the most. This quantifies your feelings so you can see how big an issue it is for you, and so you can measure your progress (we'll do this step again at the end). I asked the men what number they would give it. Several people said it was a 10. Dudley, barely looking up, said, "It's no big deal. I give it a 5." This didn't ring true to me, since it was his statement to begin with. I asked him how strongly he felt he shouldn't be here when it *was* a big deal, like when he was cleaning toilets and missing his daughter's birthday. "Then it's a 10," he said. *That's* how you do this step. You want to put yourself mentally in the place when you most strongly experienced this thought.

In Step 2, you're typically looking for ratings of 7 or higher. You wouldn't work on, say, "I shouldn't have a hangnail," and circle a 3. If you're below a 7, you would find a different issue to work on, because the point here is to work on the things that you experience as stressful. In the case of the first worksheet at Phoenix House, everyone in that room experienced a great deal of stress related to the thought "I shouldn't be here," so they all circled 10.

2 How strongly do you feel this belief to be true?

0   1   2   3   4   5   6   7   8   9   (10)

⟶ stronger

Next, in Step 3, you explore the cause-and-effect relationship between what you believe, how you feel, and how you act. This step is broken up into two parts and looks like this:

3a How do you *feel* when you believe this?
(Circle below or add your own.)

afraid   abandoned   angry   annoyed   anxious

confused   depressed   desperate   embarrassed

frustrated   helpless   hopeless   hurt   impatient

inadequate   insecure   invisible   jealous   nervous

rejected   resentful   tense   upset   worried

3b How do you *act* when you feel this way?
(Circle below or add your own.)

argue   belittle   blame   bully   complain   cry   drink

eat   escape   fight   find fault with   give up   gossip

insult   interrupt   lose sleep   manipulate   obsess

overwork   pity myself   preach   pretend   procrastinate

shop   shut down   smoke   suffer   withdraw   yell

Step 3a seems easy to some people, but for others it's a little more slippery. When I started teaching ActivInsight in 2004, I didn't have a list of words for people to look over and circle. Participants simply wrote in how they felt. Then I worked with a group of executives at a conference, and one participant surprised me by asking how he was supposed to know what feelings he felt. I realized that, for some people, identifying their feelings required a little coaching, so I included a list of emotions to choose from.

We started with 3a. I asked the men how they felt when they thought "I shouldn't be here." Angry? Then they would circle "angry." Depressed? They would circle "depressed." You'll notice there are no happy feelings, because you're working on issues that you find stressful. "I shouldn't be here" didn't make these men feel relaxed and joyful. It might make them feel something negative that's not on the list, though, in which case they would just write it in. You want to find at least three feelings that are true for you, but circling more is encouraged. Sometimes people circle almost the whole list. The point is to be honest and thorough.

After 3a, you move to 3b and ask yourself, how do you act when you feel this way? For example, when you feel angry, do you yell? Do you smoke, or drink, or eat certain foods? Look over at Step 3b and you'll see a list of behaviors. I asked the group how they felt and acted when they thought, "I shouldn't be here." Take a look at the complete list of feelings and behaviors they identified.

3a How do you *feel* when you believe this?

(Circle below or add your own.)

afraid   abandoned   (angry)   annoyed   anxious

confused   (depressed)   desperate   (embarrassed)

(frustrated) (helpless) (hopeless)   hurt   impatient

inadequate   insecure   invisible   (jealous)   nervous

rejected   (resentful)   (tense)   upset   worried

3b How do you *act* when you feel this way?

(Circle below or add your own.)

(argue)   belittle   (blame) (bully) (complain)   cry   drink

eat   escape   (fight)   find fault with   give up   gossip

(insult)   interrupt   lose sleep   manipulate   obsess

overwork   (pity myself)   preach   (pretend) (procrastinate)

shop   (shut down) (smoke) (suffer)   withdraw   yell

Step 3 isn't meant to be particularly hard, and it isn't meant to be transformational. It's meant to be revealing.

Emotional and behavioral techniques try to modify how you feel and how you act, but they overlook the fact that your emotions and behaviors don't come out of nowhere. They come from your thoughts. Step 3 makes this visible. You can see that when you believe *x*, you feel *y*, and when you feel *y*, you do *z*. You see cause and effect in black-and-white made tangible through the written word. The men at Phoenix House had been trying to stop getting high, smoking, fighting, and blaming others, but they had never before looked at where these behaviors came from. Finally, we were moving toward the source.

Metaphorically speaking, ActivInsight flips a switch in your mind from on to off. This flipping takes place in these next two steps. Step 4 asks you to negate the statement you started with in Step 1. Don't be put off by the word *negate,* drawn from formal logic. All you do is flip the main verb from negative to positive or positive to negative. I ask for the negation instead of the opposite because if the original statement is "He should love me more" and I asked you for an opposite, you might say, "He should hate me more." But that's not what we want. The correct negation for "He should love me more" is "He should not love me more." Here are some more examples:

"She shouldn't have said that" is negated to "She should have said that."

"I want a dog" is negated to "I don't want a dog."

"We need to win" is negated to "We don't need to win."

"He's a jerk" is negated to "He's not a jerk."

"I'm a failure" is negated to "I'm not a failure."

Once you've flipped the main verb, you're almost done with this step. The last part is adding a qualifier so that having an insight will be a little easier. This usually involves adding the words *In reality* at the beginning of the negation and *at this time* at the end if you're referring to the present or *at that time* if you're referring to the past. You don't do this in every case—there are variations for some statements—but as a general rule this is helpful. Here are some examples of completed negations to make this clearer:

"He should appreciate me more" becomes "In reality, he should not appreciate me more at this time."

"That shouldn't have happened" becomes "In reality, that should have happened at that time."

"I need more money" becomes "In reality, I don't need more
money at this time."

"She should listen to me" becomes "In reality, she should not listen to me at this time."

I'm sure you get the hang of it. You flip the main verb from positive to negative or negative to positive, then add *In reality* at the beginning and in most cases *at this time* or *at that time* at the end.

So what's the negation for "I shouldn't be here"? If you said, "In reality, I should be here at this time," you are correct. And if you think that the men at Phoenix House had a big problem with that statement, you are correct again.

The negation seemed like the least helpful statement we could have possibly come up with. Wasn't I there to teach them how to live with less stress? Suddenly the stress level shot through the roof! And you may already be thinking about negations for some of the issues in your life and feeling something similar. ("In reality, I should *not* weigh less at this time"!?) So take a deep breath, and let me tell you what happened.

First, I explained to these men that their resistance was actually a very good sign. And it is. It means that you're reaching the place where stress is actually created in your mind. Think about this for a second. If ActivInsight simply confirmed the statements you already believed ("I shouldn't be here" or "I should weigh less," for example), you would feel no resistance because you agree. But you would also experience no insight and would continue feeling stress. Insight by its nature involves the emergence of new information, so it's inherently challenging. And if you're open to that, it can lead to a very different experience than the one you've been stuck in. As Einstein said, "You can't solve a problem with the same mind that created it." You have to be open to seeing something new, and that means you have to be willing to challenge your own beliefs even though they seem undeniably true.

So I asked these men if they were open to having an insight, and they all said yes. They then wrote down on the lines of Step 4, "In reality, I should be here at this time." Dudley muttered under his breath that he didn't even want to make his hand write it, but they all did:

---

4 Write the negation of your statement from Step 1. In most cases, you also add "In reality" at the beginning and "at this time" or "at that time" at the end.

> *In reality, I should be here at this time.*

_____

_____

Step 4 puts your hand right on the switch you want to flip. Step 5 is where you flip it.

Flipping it involves proving that the negated statement is true. I suggested that the group imagine themselves as lawyers or as objective scientists whose sole job is to prove why these men *should* be here in reality at this time. What could they come up with?

There was a moment of dead silence. This is almost always the case when you're new to ActivInsight and you're asked to prove the negation. It just seems so unprovable. Then Jeff laughed and said, "In reality, I *should* be here at this time because the judge sent me here."

"Yes," I said. "Good. Write that down." He did.

Then Dave said sarcastically, "In reality, I *should* be here at this time because if I walk out the door now, I'll be sent back to prison." (He was mandated to be there and couldn't leave until his term was up.)

"That's also good," I said. "Write it down." He did.

Manny added with a smile, "In reality, I should be here at this time because I did drugs and got arrested."

"Yes," I said. They all wrote that down.

Elwood went next. "In reality, I should be here at this time because I ignored the judge's warnings."

Little by little, they began fleshing it out and adding to their worksheets. Here's what they came up with. See if you can sense how it got progressively deeper and more honest:

5 Write below all the proof you can find that supports the negation being true in reality at this time (or in the past). Don't rush. Be thorough, using an additional sheet of paper if necessary.

> *In reality, I should be here at this time because the judge sent me here.*

> *In reality, I should be here at this time because if I walk out the door now, I'll be sent back to prison.*

> *In reality, I should be here at this time because I did drugs and got arrested.*

> *In reality, I should be here at this time because I ignored the judge's warnings.*

> *In reality, I should be here at this time because I did things they don't even know about.*

> _In reality, I should be here at this time because I was hurting myself and people around me._

> _In reality, I should be here at this time because I was screwing up my life, and this is where society sends people to get help._

> _In reality, I should be here at this time because I need to turn my life around._

Can you see what happened? The negation had started out seeming absurd. Of course they shouldn't be here! That was the switch set to on, where stress is a 10. But as they explored the negation, they slowly began to see how it was actually true in reality, just in this moment. This is what flipping the switch off requires. You have to see what you hadn't. That's what _insight_ means: _seeing in_ to the situation more clearly. The more you see into it, the more change takes place.

Dudley, who had been very resistant at the start, came up with those last two proofs. He looked at me with eyes I'll never forget and said, "Damn. This asks you to get real. I mean, to get _really_ real, to own up to the truth." That's exactly right. ActivInsight asks you to get _really_ real, but it doesn't do this through advice or lecturing. If I had _told_ them to "get real" and finally admit that they should all be there—something that many family members, counselors, and probation officers had done—they would have gone into defense and fought me just as they'd fought everyone else, strengthening their belief that they shouldn't be there. But because I'm not a therapist, I don't have any authority to tell people anything. I also don't have any interest in doing that, because I know the power of insight. This process gives people space and guidance to look at a situation for themselves. As a result, even very resistant people can open up to see things that they had previously missed. And that is the heart of transformation.

We took in this list as a group for a few minutes, reading out loud what they had come up with to see if there was any additional proof for the negation. Reading the proof to yourself is important, because it gives you a chance to take in all the evidence at once, and reading it out loud is even more effective as you hear yourself say it. The men at Phoenix House were surprised that what had seemed such an absurd statement just a few minutes earlier now seemed obvious. That's how you know you've finished Step 5 and the switch has been flipped—the negation rings true. With practice, this happens faster and more convincingly.

Next, we moved on to Step 6, which asks you to identify the feelings that come from the negated statement. When they saw that in reality they *should* be there at this time, they reported feeling calm, clear, honest, humble, peaceful, and understanding. Dave added that he was grateful, because if he hadn't been admitted to Phoenix House, he would probably be dead. He said that, until that moment, this hadn't fully occurred to him. They circled their feelings in Step 6a, like this:

6a How do you *feel* when you see the truth of the negation? (Circle below or add your own.)

calm   clear   compassionate   connected   curious
enlightened   enthusiastic   excited   free   grateful
honest   humble   intimate   light   loving   optimistic
peaceful   playful   relaxed   relieved   serene
supportive   tolerant   truthful   understanding

Then on the right side of Step 6a, in 6b, the worksheet asks how you might act when feeling this way. When you feel calm and clear, for example, what actions could come from that? Is there something you would do, or stop doing? They thought it over, and talked about apologizing to people they had mistreated, accepting the consequences of their actions, participating in house activities, and finding jobs. They seemed sincerely excited by what they might do going forward. Here's what Step 6b looked like when they completed it:

6b What **actions** might come from this?
(Circle below or add your own.)

accept   apologize   approach   be honest   breathe
clarify   communicate   contribute   delegate   exercise
explore   focus   follow through   forgive   give thanks
listen   make amends   network   open up   participate
prioritize   reach out   share   speak up   support

find a job

You'll notice that they wrote in "find a job." If the feelings you feel or the actions you can come up with aren't on the list, you write them in. The words on the page are just suggestions to help you get started.

You'll also notice that Step 6b has dotted lines around it. This process is called ActivInsight for two reasons. First, it makes having an insight an active, step-by-step process instead of a passive one. And second, it prompts you to come up with action steps so that you can do something with what you realized. Some people cut out the action steps and tape them to their desks or schedule the action steps on their calendars. The men at Phoenix House each kept a folder and notebook and reviewed their worksheets during the week. Then they would tell me what they had done when we met again.

The last step, Step 7, simply asks you to rate the *original* belief again (not the negation). It's often helpful to add the qualifying phrase "in reality at this time" or "in reality at that time" to the original statement so your mind stays focused on the implied meaning. I asked the men how strongly they now felt that they *shouldn't* be here in reality at this time. Manny and Jeff said there was still a lingering sense of it being true and gave it a 5. Dave and Elwood gave it a 3 and 1, respectively. And Dudley, who was very much a 10 when we started, shook his head in amazement and said that if he was honest about what was true in reality right now, it was a 0—he really *should* be at Phoenix House at this time given everything that led to this moment. I've circled 3 as their average.

7 Read your original statement again. How strongly do you feel this belief to be true now?

0   1   2   ③   4   5   6   7   8   9   10

weaker ⟵————————

The difference between Step 2 and Step 7 is called the point drop. Often the first worksheets involve a very small point drop, say, 10 to 9 or 10 to 8, or even no point drop at all if you don't yet understand how the negation works. In that case, you may want to try a less charged topic, and make sure you're clear on what Step 5 is asking you to do. Keep in mind that you're not condoning anything, nor are you suggesting that you want things to remain this way. You're simply focusing your attention on the truth as it appears in a single moment. When you do this sincerely, the point drop increases with practice. It's like a muscle that hasn't been stretched before and becomes flexible little by little. Soon you'll start at 10 and end at 3 or lower every time. These men did better than most newcomers because they got "really real," as Dudley said, and were willing to see the truth of their situation.

The effect of the insight was dramatic. Previously, all five men had solidly believed that they shouldn't be there, and as a result they were angry and bitter, and they acted that out. Afterward, they could see why in reality they *should* be there right then, and they felt and behaved very differently. Dudley's change was so remarkable that the other residents of the house wanted to join our group and try ActivInsight for themselves.

And that was just our first session. Over the weeks that followed, we worked through a wide range of other issues that bothered the men and that used to provoke them to use drugs. The more worksheets we did, the lighter the men felt and the less attractive drugs became. One of the more memorable worksheets was on "Selling drugs was easy money." (It doesn't use "should" or "shouldn't," but as you'll see in part 2, not every worksheet will.) Dudley gave this a 10 when he started, fondly remembering the huge roll of cash he used to carry and the things he could buy for his family. But after proving the negation ("In reality, selling drugs was not easy money at that time") and seeing all the ways in which the negation was true—crazed addicts, competition with other dealers, shootings, drug busts, the constant fear that he would go to jail and never see his kids again—Dudley gave it a 0 and said now that he really thought about it clearly, selling drugs had been incredibly hard, and for the first time in years he was looking forward to going back to his job in construction. Several of the men said that if it hadn't been for insights like this, they felt sure they would have returned to prison. And I'm happy to say that at the time of this writing Phoenix House is now exploring making ActivInsight available nationally for all its residents in recovery.

Perhaps you already see how ActivInsight provokes transformation in an accessible new way. Or perhaps you recognize that it worked at Phoenix House, but are less clear about how this translates to the stress in your life. It may seem like there's an enormous difference between addicts in recovery coming to terms with their situation and the issues you're facing. Don't worry. In part 2, we're going to explore common issues like relationships, money, success, and weight loss so you can see how this applies to more familiar topics. But before we roll up our sleeves, there's one question we still need to address.

The myth of stress claims that stress comes from your external environment and that changes in this environment over time are causing you—and everyone—to experience greater stress today. In short, there are far more stressors now than there ever were before. But if stressors don't really exist and stress is produced internally, how do we explain what's going on? Why are we experiencing so much more stress than people used to?

In the next chapter I'm going to answer this question and explain how stress and ActivInsight really work. To do this, we have to turn the clock back long before Hans Selye came on the scene, and long before saber-toothed tigers roamed the grassy plains. Let's take a brief journey together into Earth's ancient past so you can see for yourself how stress was born.

CHAPTER 3

The Birth
of Stress

Three and a half billion years ago, when the first microscopic life forms appeared in the churning sulfurous oceans of early Earth, they had challenges to face. Well, maybe not "face," as these life forms didn't have faces back then. But when the water temperature skyrocketed, or the amount of available light plummeted, most of the very first earthlings perished. Only those microbes that happened to be a little more adaptable survived and multiplied.

This precarious state of affairs lasted for an inconceivably long two billion years. During this time, Earth's single-celled residents greatly strengthened their powers of adaptability. Then, in an unprecedented act of symbiotic cooperation, some of these microbes joined together, forming multicelled organisms. And after another billion or so years of tumbling through the seas, some of these multicelled organisms, in turn, evolved into simple animals.

This was followed by the rise of predators, roughly five hundred million years ago—not dinosaurs, but flatworms (you have to start somewhere). The flatworms' even tinier prey had no defenses, because animals had never needed defenses before. Some escaped being eaten purely due to random advantages such as the ability to swim faster, or a thicker shell, and they passed along these advantages to their offspring. Predators, too, passed on their own advantages in finding prey. Over generations, this led to more sophisticated survival strategies for creatures both on offense and defense, and eventually (in this very simplified account) to the accumulation of specialized nerve cells that could store survival-related information more effectively. In short, animals evolved brains. And for the first time on Earth, after four billion years, life could think.

Thinking shouldn't be overrated just because some of us do it today. For most of Earth's past, life had no need to think. Stimulus and response worked just fine and was a very resource-efficient way of adapting to changes. But thinking animals had an edge: not only could they react to sensory perceptions, but they could also remember the past and plan for the future. And as thinking developed further, animals began to organize social structures and pool resources, further favoring their survival. Even though these new brains required a good deal of energy, they proved to be valuable, and over time they became larger.

In the special case of our hominid ancestors, larger brains led to further conceptual capacity, which led to more use and greater advantage, which led to still larger brains. It was a feedback loop, which biologist Christopher Wills has called a "runaway brain." As a result, a much higher level of thinking emerged.

And so did stress.

Remember that the myth of stress claimed that stress exists because of external changes—over the past few million years, the world has become a faster, flatter, more complicated place, and instead of just the occasional saber-toothed tiger, we're now surrounded by countless stressors every day. It's true that the world has changed, but the real reason we experience more stress involves changes that took place not in our environment, but in our heads.

Consider this: Six million years ago our ancestors' brains measured around twenty-four cubic inches, roughly the size of a modern chimpanzee's brain. Today the average human brain measures ninety cubic inches. That's more than triple the size. But size was not the only change. Some parts of our brain grew more than the rest. The part that grew the most is the neocortex, the gray, wrinkly, outer layer that makes mammalian brains look so distinctively brainlike. The neocortex is responsible for abstract higher functions like conceptual thought.

Human beings today do not have the world's biggest brains (those belong to Sperm whales), but we do have the greatest brain-to-body-size ratio, and the greatest proportion of neocortex. This gives us an enormous capacity for abstract thought. The fact that as your eyes move across the markings on this page you can easily translate them into intelligible information is a testament to your neocortex, which possesses pretty remarkable abilities that no other species on Earth shares.

What does this mean? Over the past few million years, the human brain has evolved into the world's most sophisticated abstract-thinking machine. But abstract thinking alone isn't problematic. After all, you can read words or do math in your head (each a feat of abstraction) without experiencing stress. Stress is produced by a particular kind of abstract thinking, something that linguists and social psychologists call *counterfactual thought.*

"Counterfactual thought" is a fancy way of saying something very familiar. Have you ever had a thought such as "If I weighed less, I would be more attractive"? How about "If I had more money, my life would be easier"? These are examples of counterfactual thinking. The first part of the statement counters the facts of life as they actually are. Linguists would limit the term *counterfactual* to conditional "if" sentences like these, but I'm going to rebelliously expand it to include any statement that "counters the facts" of life. For example, if I think, "I should be eight feet tall," and I'm not eight feet tall, I'm thinking counterfactually, because this thought counters the facts as they actually are. This is a radical definition of counterfactuality, and it plays a crucial part in understanding how stress works and how ActivInsight works as well.

The things appearing to your senses right now—these words as you read them, the sounds taking place around you, the feeling of clothes on your skin—these are factual reality. All living creatures experience this in one form or another through the senses. Each of the five senses that we humans use most (taste, touch, sight, sound, and smell) is more developed in other species. Eagles can spot a mouse in high grass from over a mile away. Bloodhounds can smell a drop of gasoline in ten gallons of water. Compared to animals like these, our senses are primitive.

If we consider thought a kind of sixth sense, however, we humans excel in it and far outstrip other animals. And thought has one key difference. The other senses are inextricably bound to present experience. You can't smell something in the future or taste something in the past. Thought, however, isn't tied to immediate experience, and gives humans the rare ability to tune out what's going on in factual reality and essentially travel in time—to shift our attention away from how things are to how things "should" be, or how they used to be, or how we're afraid they might be. Who hasn't imagined a different job, a different body, a different hand from the one he or she was dealt? Some people spend most of their lives adrift in beliefs about what could or should have been and are hardly aware that they're doing something special. What they *are* aware of, though, is the stress.

As I mentioned earlier, the emotional experience of stress doesn't come from your job, your body, your family, your love life, your finances, or your responsibilities. Physical challenges such as fatigue and pain may come from these things, but the emotional burden of stress comes from the act of thinking itself, from the lightning-fast comparisons taking place in your subconscious mind between what really is and your counterfactual belief about what "should" or "shouldn't" be. Every time you experience stress, you're thinking counterfactually. In fact, it's not possible to experience stress without thinking counterfactually.

Historically, this began as a very helpful ability. For example, consider a thought like, "Glugg should not have poked mammoth." That thought may have been painful, but it had real survival value. An even older example of counterfactual thought would be something like, "Tiger going to kill me." At first this may seem to be purely factual. At the moment you think it, however, you don't really know that it's true. All you see factually is a tiger running toward you. That may sound absurd because we're all so used to the immediate jump into counterfactual thinking and the corresponding fight-or-flight response, but even the most automatic responses to threats (and the concept of threat itself) are by-products of thought and have been learned through exposure over millennia.

The fight-or-flight mechanism that we take for granted today originally occurred when a counterfactual thought provoked a response in the brain, which then triggered a release of stress hormones in the body and reflexes that led to the animal's escape from possible injury or death—a worthwhile trade-off. The short-term emotional and physical burden of stress is offset by the greater likelihood of long-term survival.

So if stress offers a survival advantage, why not keep it? The main reason is that times have changed. The stress that most humans experience today offers no survival advantages. In fact, just the opposite is true—experiencing stress damages your body and leads to a long list of diseases including high blood pressure, heart disease, chronic pain and fatigue, and depression, which shorten your life. If your main interest is in living happily and not in fleeing predators, you'll want to lessen the amount of stress you experience, and that means learning to identify your counterfactual thoughts and challenge them.

I want to point out here that while all stress comes from counterfactual thinking, not all counterfactual thinking produces stress. It's helpful to distinguish between two types of counterfactual thought. The first type I'll call "expansive." Expansive thoughts give your mind wings and make you feel wonderful—think of a big project you're excited by, a vacation you're planning, a special someone you can't stop thinking about. These types of thoughts are all made possible by your neocortex's ability to counterfactually depart from "this" and envision "that." What could be more human, and more inspiring? You don't need to work on expansive beliefs and the positive emotions they create. Just enjoy them.

On the other hand, negative emotions like frustration, anger, sadness, and fear exist on the flip side of counterfactuality. Rather than expanding your mind and raising you up to a higher level of joy, these contract you. Contractive thoughts pull you down into a spiral of anxiety and depression and are the kind of counterfactual thinking that produces stress.

When you experience a physical contraction, like a muscle spasm, you know that something is wrong, and you might see a massage therapist who applies gentle pressure to break up the contraction and restore flow to the area. I want you to think of stress as involving something similar, but taking place in your mind instead of your body. Just as a physical contraction produces physical pain, a mental contraction produces mental pain. This stress tells you that there has been a disruption in your subconscious thought process and that your mind has contracted away from the flow of life as it is. Stress isn't a bad thing, just as pain isn't a bad thing. They're both important signals.

The more stress you have in your life, the more contracted beliefs you have in your subconscious mind (about money, success, love, etc.). We've been taught that different emotional states are produced by different circumstances, but the truth is that your emotions are produced by your beliefs. This is why different people can be exposed to the exact same circumstances (such as public speaking) and have very different experiences. One person might have a belief that this is a dangerous situation, which leads to a strong contraction and stress. Another person, believing it's an opportunity, would be unfazed, and another might even find the situation enjoyable.

If you've ever seen people who remain calm during so-called stressful situations, you might have wondered what they're doing that you're not. But the real question to ask is, What are *you* doing that *they're* not? And the answer is that you're believing certain counterfactual thoughts. A stress-free life isn't about trying to stay calm. Calm is your baseline state, and you contract away from it through false beliefs. From this perspective, the opposite of stress is not relaxation. The opposite of stress is education, releasing the contractions by having insights.

Releasing contracted thoughts through insight is completely natural. When a child is scared of monsters in the dark, you don't teach him to relax, breathe, or cope. You turn on the lights. That quickly helps him see that what he had believed to be true ("There's a monster") is actually false ("In reality, there's no monster at this time"). The same thing happens naturally over time to other beliefs that children have, such as "Kissing is gross." Through their own experience, they learn to see that the belief is false, and as a result the stress falls away and the behavior changes.

The difficulty with gaining insight through experience, however, is that it can take years. The seven steps of the ActivInsight process help you provoke an insight *now*. And the more directly you can pinpoint the core of the contraction in your mind, the more powerful the insight will be. This is why we generally use the words *should* or *shouldn't* on our worksheet—they are the most concentrated form of contracted counterfactual thinking. They are a direct violation of reality. Of course, before the insight, we think our "should" statements are true ("I should weigh less," "I should be more successful," etc.), and that *reality* is the violation. Our contracted beliefs seem so undeniably correct to us. This is further testament to the abstract capability of the human neocortex and would be amusing if it didn't have such tragic consequences for our well-being.

In addition to the structure of our brains, culture and language also influence our beliefs. Even with the same neocortex, a culture using a very different language may see their world less counterfactually and experience less stress as a result. In the book *Don't Sleep, There Are Snakes,* linguist Daniel L. Everett describes his time among the Pirahan tribe in the Amazon, whose members have very little counterfactuality in their language or culture and are the happiest people Everett and his fellow linguists have ever encountered. The Hopi language and culture seem to share a similar grounding in factual reality and peace of mind.

But you, as a modern Westerner, come from a culture and a linguistic system with strong counterfactual tendencies, and consequently you will most likely resist defining "should" as what's real. You want to define "should" in terms of the ideal: "People shouldn't wage war." "Children shouldn't tell lies." "Spouses should be faithful." The structure of the idealized "should" is tightly woven into your value system and your morality. That's how you were educated to see the world.

This isn't right, wrong, good, or bad. It's just how things are. But if you're interested in living without stress, you need to challenge this structure. As you do more ActivInsight, little by little your mind reconnects to factual reality, the counterfactual "should" starts to break down, and you come to the simple truth that what "should" be right now is what actually is—"should is"—

and the proof for this is *the entire history of life on Earth leading up to this moment.* This may be incomprehensible at first because your mind is so used to flying off into the counterfactual "should." You initially reject the idea that "should is," and believe that saying "should is" will lead to immorality, passivity, and the condoning of unacceptable things.

To get past this, it's essential to realize that by recognizing that "should is," you're not wishing that a situation *remain* the way it is. You're not saying you *want* people to wage war and you *want* spouses to cheat. ActivInsight is not prescriptive. It's *descriptive.* You're seeing reality as it is *so that you can create change,* but you can do it with open eyes and a more peaceful mind instead of with denial and anger.

In other words, you're not negating your goals. You're negating the contracted beliefs that keep you from achieving your goals more easily, because these beliefs produce feelings and behaviors that work against you. When you say, "Children shouldn't lie," you become angry, which makes your children afraid of you, so they keep lying. But when you say that "In reality, children should lie at this time" *and then prove to yourself how and why this is true,* you start to see the world as it is and can find more intelligent and compassionate ways to change it. You are not condoning anything. You're seeing life realistically so that you can be even more effective at transforming it.

To make this switch from the counterfactual "should" to the reality-based "should," you have to lean heavily on the qualifying words. *In reality* gently pulls you back to Earth, and *at this time* reminds you that we're just talking about today, not the future. Then you have to prove the negation in Step 5. The other steps are built around the insights of the proved negation.

People often ask why we don't make things simpler and avoid the word *should* altogether. Instead of the men at Phoenix House saying, "In reality, I *should* be here at this time," which seems at first to be so wrong, why not say, "In reality, I *am* here at this time" and have someone prove that? The reason is that it doesn't address the core contraction. Someone who says, "I am here at this time" still feels that he *shouldn't* be, just as someone who says, "I don't weigh less at this time" still feels that she *should*. As long as that "should" remains buried in your mind, you will experience stress. What you need to do is not avoid your "shoulds," but dismantle them.

The reason that sounds scary is because you believe that the "should" is what motivates you to change. "If I don't believe I *should* weigh less," you think, "I'll never lose the weight." "If I don't believe I *should* be more successful, I won't work hard to get ahead." This is simply not true. Seeing reality as it is removes the contraction from your mind and lets you focus on your goals *without* the emotional upheaval and the negative behaviors that come with it. It's a lot easier to work late or eat right when you're feeling clearheaded than when you're feeling anxious and inadequate.

The idea that stress fuels you and that peace turns you into a doormat is pervasive. It's time to set the record straight and help you see how much more energy you have when you're not bogged down by anxiety, confusion, anger, and fear. And the only way to really do this is to experience the power of insight for yourself.

So that's what we're going to do now. You've seen how the myth of stress was created during Hans Selye's reign, you've witnessed the evolution of the human brain and its abstract-thinking capacities, and you've learned how contracted counterfactual thinking produces stress and how insight can dissolve it. Now we're going to apply ActivInsight to a wide range of common challenges so you can begin eliminating the stress in your life. Let's get started.

PART TWO

INSIGHT IN ACTION

INTRODUCTION
TO PART TWO

In part 2, we're going to work together on twelve commonly stressful issues, including money, success, interpersonal conflict, weight loss, and more. As we go forward, it's helpful if you think of ActivInsight as a kind of exercise program. Instead of losing physical weight, though, you'll be losing mental weight. And instead of building physical flexibility, you're going to build your mental flexibility and resilience.

In a physical exercise program, you don't do every exercise at once. The same applies here. The best way to get value from part 2 is to do one chapter at a time, pausing to integrate and reflect on each exercise. Try to do at least three chapters a week (though if you feel able to move faster, go ahead). We'll start with fairly easy topics and build to harder ones as we go along. It's important that you not skip ahead. The topics are arranged in order so that by the time we get to the harder topics, you're ready for them.

Some people have breakthroughs from the very first worksheet, but for others the initial attempts can sometimes lead to a disappointing sense that what we're doing is just playing with words in our heads and justifying people's behaviors. This is not the case. Continuing with the sports analogy, think of the first time you tried to ride a bike and fell, or the first time you swung at a golf ball and missed completely. ActivInsight is a skill, and like any skill, some people take to it right away, but most need a little more time to feel that they're truly getting it. If you keep practicing and sincerely work through each topic in the pages ahead, the steps of ActivInsight will make more and more sense, you'll get better at them, and you'll soon notice profound changes taking place in your thought process and, even more important, in your life.

We're going to prove that all the saber-toothed tigers or stressors in your life were never really out there. They were in here, in your head. But they don't look like tigers. Here is what they really look like for the typical stressed-out person:

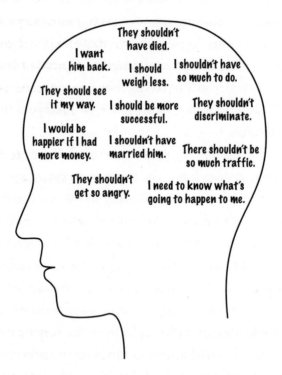

Stress is a by-product of contracted thoughts. You can't see these thoughts, but you can certainly feel them in your mind and in your body. They may seem to disappear when you exercise, have a drink, get a massage, or think positively, but they remain in place deeper in the mind. Like weeds cut just at the surface, their roots remain intact, so they soon reemerge. With ActivInsight, we go for the roots.

In the chapters that follow, we're going to explore all the topics in that head above, using the same seven steps for each topic. If this seems repetitive, that's because it is. Every time you experience stress, your mind is doing the same thing—it's contracting away from reality in the same way. Consequently, every time you do ActivInsight, you reconnect your mind to reality in the same way. ActivInsight is repetitive by design. Give yourself time between worksheets so that you can refresh your energy and remind yourself of your goal—less stress, greater insight, and a happier life.

For our first topic, we'll tackle something that isn't too threatening but is still stressful for millions of people around the world. Print out a worksheet, get a pen, and buckle your seat belt. We're heading into traffic.

CHAPTER 4

The Myth
of Traffic

Traffic is regularly listed as one of the top stressors of modern life. In reality, of course, traffic is not a stressor. It's your thoughts about traffic, not the traffic itself, that produce whatever stress you experience.

This is easy enough to prove. The next time you're in a traffic jam, take a look around you at the typical behaviors taking place—people honking, cursing, and waving at each other with one finger. But keep looking and you'll see that some people appear to be only mildly frustrated, and others are listening to music and passing the time contentedly. You'll even spot a few children who appear to be fully enjoying themselves, maybe playing games in the backseats of their parents' cars.

These children are in the exact same traffic jam as the adults about to burst a blood vessel, so it makes no sense to say that traffic is a stressor. Your reaction to traffic or any other supposed stressor reflects your contracted beliefs, not your circumstances. This is why different people have widely different reactions to the same circumstances. The reaction reflects what's going on inside you, not outside.

For decades, social psychologists have tried to measure the amount of stress in someone's life by using Stressful Life Events scales. Test takers check off a list of events like traffic, divorce, a move, death of a loved one, etc., and the resulting score supposedly reveals their stress level. The problem with this approach is that it fails to capture the way people *think about* the events in their lives, which is where the stress is really created.

It may be true that most people find divorce or the death of a loved one to be very stressful experiences, but this is not a given. It's mainly the result of cultural conditioning, so a large percentage of people in the same culture or community will share the same counterfactual beliefs and the same resulting emotional experiences. But there *are* people who divorce each other amicably. There are also people who manage to move or change jobs without much ado, and who see death as a positive transformation. Proponents of Stressful Life Events scales misunderstand these differences, saying that these people have "emotional immunity" or are "insulated" somehow and "less vulnerable" to life changes, as if they have mysterious, possibly unattainable traits. This is untrue and assumes that these life events are inherently negative and that you need to be invulnerable to them or insulated from them. If something isn't stressful for you, it simply isn't stressful.

To remedy this, what if instead of measuring stress from the outside, we measured it from the inside? I don't mean inside the body by measuring hormones. I mean inside the mind by measuring beliefs.

Suppose you were to conduct a little survey, asking people who regularly experience traffic to rate on a scale from 0 to 10 (ten being the most) how strongly they believe the statement "There shouldn't be so much traffic." I've done this many times and consistently find that the people who rate this statement a 10 are the same people who get very angry behind the wheel, while those who contentedly listen to music in traffic or talk on the phone might give it a 5. People who are unfazed by traffic, like the kids in the backseat, would give it a 0 or 1. So the numerical rating indicates the strength of the belief, and the strength of the belief reveals the amount of stress someone experiences on that issue. This is a very fast and accurate way of quantifying a subjective experience.

This rating system also reveals how relative stress is. On the Life Events Scales, someone who is divorced simply checks the box saying that she got divorced. The survey doesn't reflect any sense of subjectivity. But if you ask people to rate on a scale from 0 to 10 a divorce-related belief such as "I shouldn't have married him," you find that some people rate it a 10 and others a lower number, such as a 3 or 6. We're not all equally stressed out by this belief. And when you look at other beliefs, such as those relating to money, success, and relationships, the stress people experience is relative and variable for those topics, too.

When you fully grasp this, a light goes on. It becomes possible to admit that events themselves aren't inherently and absolutely stressful, that something internal always mediates how much stress is produced. If divorce, moving, and the loss of a loved one were a 10 for everyone on Earth, this would support the concepts of stressors and Stressful Life Events, but this is never the case. For any issue you struggle greatly with, there is someone who struggles less or not at all. Everything is relative. Even the person who drives you crazy has friends. This variability proves the fact that thoughts, not events, shape your emotional experience of life. But it's not enough to know this intellectually. You have to find the specific thoughts you struggle with and directly challenge them in order to experience real change. You'll do this now by starting with the topic of traffic.

Incidentally, I hope this is obvious, but I'm not suggesting that when you're actually in traffic you should whip out a worksheet. There may be moments when you experience stress and it's not practical or safe to do ActivInsight. In those cases, use other techniques for getting through the situation (breathing, relaxation, "Serenity now"). Even just doing the negation in your head and thinking of proof can be helpful. I know one woman who does this frequently throughout her week: "In reality, my husband *should* be in a bad mood because he's exhausted. In reality, my mother-in-law *should* criticize me because she thinks she's being helpful." This mini-insight can give you a quick hit of perspective and prevent you from getting too bothered. But if the issue is still charged for you later, find time to do a complete worksheet on paper so that you have a bigger insight. Then *the next time* the situation arises, you won't have to do negations in your head. Your entire experience will be different.

Think of ActivInsight as a training tool that you use between life challenges. The beauty is that once you really get the hang of these steps, you'll find that they shift how you see an issue not just the next time, but for every time you encounter it thereafter. In other words, the more you do ActivInsight now, the less you'll need to do it in the future. In this sense, it's an investment. You invest a little time on each worksheet, and the return on your investment is the deeper peace and understanding you'll have going forward from then on. But you can't get this peace by just thinking about it. You have to actually challenge your beliefs head on.

So let's begin with a worksheet on traffic. Follow along on your own worksheet, even if traffic isn't a big deal for you, because it will help cement the skills behind each step. First, you simply state the emotional charge you feel in the form of a "should" or "shouldn't" statement:

1 Write a concise, complete sentence describing something that you experience as stressful. It's helpful to use the words "should" or "shouldn't." (Ex.: "They should listen to me.")

> *There shouldn't be so much traffic.*

Keep it short and simple. That's it for Step 1.

In Step 2, you rate your statement. Write from the place you most strongly experience the statement as true. When I first moved to Los Angeles, I pulled onto the highway around noon one day to drive to a meeting. I had assumed that there would be no traffic in the middle of the day, but the highway was practically a parking lot. At that moment, "There shouldn't be so much traffic" was a 10. See if you can write your worksheet from a similar place mentally, then circle the number that feels right to you:

2 How strongly do you feel this belief to be true?

0   1   2   3   4   5   6   7   8   9   10

━━━━━━━━━━▶ stronger

Next, in Step 3, write how you feel when you're stuck in traffic and you think, "There shouldn't be so much traffic." You may feel fine about traffic now, but when you mentally put yourself back among the slowly crawling cars when you were running late, how did you feel then? Impatient? Tense? That's how I used to feel. Look over the list and circle whatever feelings arise for you. Try to find at least three feelings in Step 3a, adding any that aren't on the list by writing them in.

3a How do you *feel* when you believe this? (Circle below or add your own.)

afraid   abandoned   angry   annoyed   anxious

confused   depressed   desperate   embarrassed

frustrated   helpless   hopeless   hurt   impatient

inadequate   insecure   invisible   jealous   nervous

rejected   resentful   tense   upset   worried

Once you've circled the related feelings in 3a, look at 3b. When you're feeling this way, what do you do? Be honest. For example, when I believe there shouldn't be so much traffic, I complain, blame others, curse, tailgate, change lanes recklessly, and then, when the traffic lightens up, speed. (Always be as thorough and honest as you can be in this step.) If you snap at your spouse or kids, or act rudely to other drivers, you want to note that. This is not about being right or wrong. It's an exercise in connecting the dots between your beliefs, your feelings, and your behaviors. You're the only one who's going to see it, so why not write the truth?

Take a few minutes to think about how you act, then capture this on your worksheet.

3b How do you *act* when you feel this way?
(Circle below or add your own.)

argue   belittle   blame   bully   complain   cry   drink

eat   escape   fight   find fault with   give up   gossip

insult   interrupt   lose sleep   manipulate   obsess

overwork   pity myself   preach   pretend   procrastinate

shop   shut down   smoke   suffer   withdraw   yell

When you're done, you should be able to see the cause-and-effect relationship between your belief (Step 1), your feelings (3a), and your behaviors (3b). Step 2 is a multiplier. The higher you rate the belief in Step 2, the stronger the feelings and behaviors are in Step 3.

Now move on to Step 4. What's the negation for "There shouldn't be so much traffic"? Remember, we add "In reality" at the beginning and usually add "at this time" or "at that time" at the end, and negate the main verb. So the correct answer is:

4 Write the negation of your statement from Step 1. In most cases, you also add "In reality" at the beginning and "at this time" or "at that time" at the end.

> *In reality, there should be so much traffic at this time.*

This statement can sound strange when you're new to Activ-Insight, but you are not saying that you want there to be traffic or that you like it. You're just looking at why, in this specific moment, there should be so much traffic in reality. It's as if time has stopped, life is frozen, and you are looking down on Earth at this curious thing called "traffic," seeing that it is there. The traffic *should* exist in reality right now, because everything happening now is the effect of prior causes.

I've sometimes been told that I'm using "should" in an unnatural way—that seeing why traffic exists right now explains why it *is* there, but not why it *should* be there. But why it is there *is* why it should be there, and separating the two onto different tracks is what produces stress.

In a sense, using "should" to point to an ideal state is unnatural. When we say things like "There shouldn't be so much traffic," we lose awareness of the natural world around us. A few million years ago, such a thought would have been literally unthinkable, as our brains were not yet as capable of abstraction. From this perspective, using "should" the way we do in ActivInsight is much *more* natural, because it brings the mind back to nature, to the real world surrounding us.

Regarding traffic, can you see how it's true that in reality at this time there *should* be so much traffic? For example, in Los Angeles, part of why there *should* be so much traffic in reality at this time is that there are millions of people living in an area served by only a few major highways. That's part of the recipe for traffic and why it should be there in reality *at this time*. In some other city, or in the Los Angeles of the future, there may be more highways, more mass transit, or fewer people, and no traffic. But today that's not the case, so it would go on your worksheet as evidence or proof of why traffic exists at this moment.

Take time now to come up with as much proof as you can for

why, in reality, there should be so much traffic at this time in your area, and write it on the lines in Step 5 of your worksheet. If there's no traffic where you live, you can work on Los Angeles or a big city near you. Be thorough. Use a blank sheet of paper if you need more room. Then continue to the paragraph below. Don't keep reading. Throughout the book, I want you to try to come up with your own proof before you read my suggestions.

Here's some possible proof for why in reality there should be so much traffic at this time. If any of it rings true to you, add it to your list. Though I'm writing about LA, similar evidence has come from people living in San Francisco, San Diego, New York, London, Hong Kong, and Dubai, with very minor changes. Traffic is traffic.

In reality, there should be so much traffic at this time because there are millions of people living in an area with only a few highways.

The first few pieces of evidence in Step 5 may seem almost *too* obvious, but by writing them down, you open yourself up to bigger insights. So writing down the obvious is okay, and even encouraged. The truth is that if there weren't so many people and so few highways, there wouldn't be so much traffic. Think about that, write it down, then go on to the next proof.

In reality, there should be so much traffic at this time because this is a car culture, and people like to drive (often alone).

Think about all the songs that glorify hitting the road in your own set of wheels. Are there any songs that glorify carpooling and taking mass transit? People today are encouraged to express their identities through their cars. It's part of our culture. We may want that to change, but it's still the case right now, so that's part of why there should be so much traffic in reality *at this time.*

In reality, there should be so much traffic at this time because options for public transportation are limited.

In New York City, I take the subway almost every day. I lived in Los Angeles for nine years, and I think I took the bus twice. I never even saw a Metro stop. This may be changing, but in the meantime limited public transportation options are part of why there should be so much traffic today in countless cities and towns. If that's true in your case, write it on your list.

In reality, there should be so much traffic at this time because the area is so large that driving is often the most convenient method of travel.

Part of why in reality there should be so much traffic at this time is because we often live relatively far from where we need to go, and a car is still the fastest way to cover ground.

Do you see how we do this step? Focus your mind on the conditions taking place in a single moment in the real world, and write down what you find. This is the proof for the negation. We're not looking for far-fetched ideas such as "In reality, there should be so much traffic at this time because humans haven't yet built a working teleporter." We're looking for more practical proof. Here is what it looks like written on the worksheet, with some additional proof included.

5 Write below all the proof you can find that supports the negation being true in reality at this time (or in the past). Don't rush. Be thorough, using an additional sheet of paper if necessary.

> In reality, there should be so much traffic at this time because there are millions of people living in an area with only a few highways.

> *In reality, there should be so much traffic at this time because this is a car culture, and people like to drive (often alone).*

> *In reality, there should be so much traffic at this time because options for public transportation are limited.*

> *In reality, there should be so much traffic at this time because the area is so large that driving is often the most convenient method of travel.*

> *In reality, there should be so much traffic at this time because driving is not heavily disincentivized.*

> *In reality, there should be so much traffic at this time because adding more highways now would be very expensive and disruptive.*

> *In reality, there should be so much traffic at this time because most people here prefer to live fairly far from where they work.*

> *In reality, there should be so much traffic at this time because I tell myself there's nothing I can do but complain, so I drive and continue to be part of the problem.*

This is a thorough effort. You want to take time to really think about why the negation is true. You're not condoning it. You just try to see it for what it is, because it's *not* seeing it that produces stress and anger. Stress always indicates a blind spot. When you can recognize reality at face value, you don't necessarily enjoy it, but you *understand* it. And that brings you a measure of peace and also improves your chances of being able to change it.

A big part of this comes with that last piece of evidence. Notice that, in the first part of Step 5, we were looking at external circumstances (highways, cars, culture) that are apparently beyond our control. Once you've done that, you look at *your* part so that you don't just point the finger outward. You want to find whatever sliver of accountability is on your plate, no matter how small it is (though in some cases it's much more than a sliver). And part of why there should be so much traffic in reality right now is that you're just like everybody else. You don't want to take the bus, ride a bike, or telecommute. You want to get in *your* car, listen to *your* music, and drive at your own convenience. So you have to write that down as a factor in the equation. Especially when you're working on other people or external conditions, you want to end Step 5 by looking at ways in which your actions or inactions play a part.

When you've finished Step 5, read the proof to yourself out loud in one pass. As you read it, take in the truth of it. When you can see why in reality at this time the negation is actually true, your work in this step is done. This may not happen fully in the beginning, but with practice it will happen more and more, and statements that had seemed absurd or impossible when you wrote them down will end up seeming almost obvious.

Next, in Step 6a, ask yourself how it feels to see the truth of the negation clearly. When you recognize all the elements contributing to traffic in this moment and admit that in reality, at this time, there *should* be so much traffic (not condoning it, but just understanding it), what do you feel? For this topic, people often circle *calm, clear, honest, humble, peaceful, relaxed, tolerant,* and *understanding.* See what feels right to you, and circle them on your worksheet.

6a How do you *feel* when you see the truth of the negation? (Circle below or add your own.)

calm   clear   compassionate   connected   curious

enlightened   enthusiastic   excited   free   grateful

honest   humble   intimate   light   loving   optimistic

peaceful   playful   relaxed   relieved   serene

supportive   tolerant   truthful   understanding

At first you may feel a lingering sense of frustration—intellectually you see the negation is true, but emotionally you still feel stress. This happens in the beginning because you still have some resistance to the negation. Do a few more worksheets and apply yourself to seeing Step 5 with as much honesty as you can, reminding yourself that you're just talking about right now, not the future. Most people find that they then experience the negation more deeply, their minds and emotions become aligned, and the feelings in Step 6a become easier to identify.

In the next part of Step 6, you imagine how you would act when you're feeling that way. What would it look like to fully realize that there *should* be so much traffic in reality at that moment? What might you do?

For example, you might leave earlier to get where you're going on time. Or, if you've just pulled onto the highway, you might exit quickly and find another route. What you don't do is sputter and curse and slap the dashboard, working yourself into a frenzy believing that there *shouldn't* be so much traffic. When you see clearly that there *should* be so much traffic at this time, you can think and act more clearly. Once I could see that, in reality, there should be so much traffic at that time, I was able to get around LA much more intelligently, and I learned which surface streets to take and which to avoid. I also came up with ways to be more productive while sitting in traffic. See what you can come up with on your worksheet.

6b What **actions** might come from this?
(Circle below or add your own.)

accept   apologize   approach   be honest   breathe

clarify   communicate   contribute   delegate   exercise

explore   focus   follow through   forgive   give thanks

listen   make amends   network   open up   participate

prioritize   reach out   share   speak up   support

The final step, Step 7, asks you to rate again the belief you started with: "There shouldn't be so much traffic." In this step, your mind may snap back to the counterfactual use of *should:* "There really shouldn't be so much traffic. It's a waste of time." But bring yourself back to the world you actually live in, not the world you're imagining. What your original statement really says is, "In reality, there shouldn't be so much traffic at this time." According to what you now know, is that true or false? Can you see that it's false in your own experience? If so, how would you rate the strength of this statement now on your worksheet?

7 Read your original statement again. How strongly do you feel this belief to be true now?

0   1   2   3   4   5   6   7   8   9   10

weaker ←————————

On the first few worksheets, most people find themselves starting at a 10 and ending somewhere between a 5 and a 7. As you continue to do more worksheets, the counterfactual "should" begins to loosen, and you'll find yourself going down further on this last step. Eventually, you won't see the original statement as true at all, because you'll define what "should" be in terms of reality instead of your imagination. But since most of us have been contracting mentally for our entire lives, this usually takes some time. It's like a muscle that has never been stretched. It just takes practice.

I've done this worksheet on "There shouldn't be so much traffic" with audiences from around the world, partly because it's now a global issue, and partly because people consider it stressful but not too personally challenging. Most people drop 3 to 5 points from Step 1 to Step 7. If you had a similar point drop, you should feel a slight shift in how you think about traffic. You'll see the effects of this shift when you're in traffic again and find yourself less bothered by it than in the past. You may still have the thought, "There shouldn't be so much traffic," quickly followed by anger, but then the negation will also follow so that the anger doesn't go as deep. For a little while, you may find yourself seeing both sides of the issue—not quite experiencing complete peace, but not experiencing real anger, either. With practice, you'll see the negation as increasingly true and the original statement as increasingly false. Then you'll circle 0 for Step 7, and the anger will be gone no matter how bad the traffic gets. You will just see life as it is, and act accordingly.

One man from Dubai, where traffic is worse than in Los Angeles, felt so excited after doing this worksheet and dropping eight points that he said he couldn't wait to go back into traffic to see it through new eyes. To him it was like a gauge that honestly reflected how well the city had planned transportation (he was a transportation engineer). A woman from San Diego realized that traffic wasn't an aberration that destroyed an otherwise peaceful commute—it *was* her commute. Consequently, she began listening to audiobooks and recovering time she had previously wasted in frustration. Insights can liberate energy that had been stuck for years.

If you went down just one or two points or didn't go down at all, don't worry. You're going to do more worksheets on different topics, and the steps will get clearer. Different examples resonate more strongly for different people. We're just getting started.

This worksheet helps demonstrate that the idea of traffic as a stressor is a myth. Traffic can't cause stress. Thoughts about traffic cause stress, and when those thoughts shift, the stress shifts, even if the traffic itself stays the same. This happens not through affirmations, willpower, forced acceptance, justification, or choice. It happens when you realize that what you had assumed to be true is actually false in this moment.

This dynamic of transformation through insight applies to any stressful issue. Next we'll take on another myth—the myth of anger—as something that you can manage. You may want to take a break before the next chapter so that you're feeling fresh. You'll need two things before we get started: another blank worksheet and someone in your life who you think overreacts in anger. You can get the worksheet at mythofstress.com. The angry person is not included.

CHAPTER 5

The Myth
of Anger

If you live or work with an angry person, this chapter is for you. Maybe it's your boss, or your partner. Maybe it's a parent or friend. But there's something you can do to deal with the situation short of buying a tranquilizer gun. You can learn to see anger in a startlingly different light. And, surprisingly, this will help the angry person as well.

This ability to help others by first helping yourself is reflected in something I call the ActivInsight SPIRAL. I'm sure you've heard people say that someone's life is spiraling out of control. But you can also spiral the other way, away from stress and confusion up toward peace of mind. The ActivInsight SPIRAL is a mnemonic device that describes six steps along this upward path. Before we work on the issue of someone else's anger, I want to share the SPIRAL stages with you to illustrate why working on your beliefs about others enables you to help them. Here's the SPIRAL with all the stages spelled out:

The ActivInsight SPIRAL

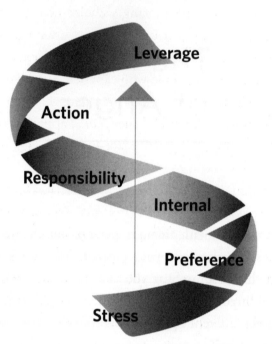

As you might have guessed, the *S* at the bottom of the SPIRAL stands for Stress. When you feel stress, that feeling is telling you that you've mentally contracted away from reality into an emotionally disconnected state. Of course, no one likes feeling this way. You want to know how to pick yourself up. The first step is simply to acknowledge that you're experiencing stress.

Then the next step up is *P,* which stands for Preference. Do you prefer stress or happiness? That may sound like a no-brainer, so let me ask it another way. Do you prefer being right or being at peace? So many of us are determined to be right, and we defend our positions with the skill of a lawyer and the stubbornness of a mule. If you're good at this, you may get to continue being right for years and everyone will know it, but the cost is your peace of mind.

Looking over your life today, can you see areas in which you fight to be right, even though it causes you stress? There's a way out of this, but it requires making a choice first. So, do you prefer being right or being at peace? I know, you want to be right *and* be at peace, but that is not an option. You can choose only one. Which will it be? Most people who experience stress remain at the bottom of the SPIRAL because of their determination to be right ("I *should* be more successful." "They *should* appreciate me more"). If you are wise enough to prefer peace—even though it may mean that you're wrong—you move up to the next step.

This is the letter *I*, which stands for Internal. Do you fully recognize that stress is an internally produced experience? Or are you still blaming other people for your anger or pain? If you think that others stress you out, that someone else has the power to hurt you or make you feel a certain way, then you may prefer peace, but you won't go any higher. I'm not saying that people don't do terrible things, and this isn't about letting them off the hook. This is about simply seeing that no matter what happens to you, that experience by itself can't produce your emotions. There has to be an intermediary step in your own thought process. Without that step, the experience would fade into the past as any other sensory experience does. Experiences can only touch your emotions and linger through thought.

Most people go through their entire lives without clearly understanding the relationship between thought and emotions, and without realizing that the source of all emotions (positive and negative) is internal. Nothing can make you frustrated. Nothing can make you depressed. Nothing can make you angry. For that matter, nothing can make you happy, either. All your emotions are produced from your own mental interpretations.

This contradicts what many people believe. Just as the world seems flat but is actually not, it seems like your emotions come from your circumstances. But if you can see through this illusion and recognize that stress is produced internally, not externally, you're ready to go further up the SPIRAL.

We're halfway up the SPIRAL now, up to the *R*, which stands for Responsibility. Let's say you recognize that you experience Stress. You Prefer peace, even if it means you don't get to be right. You fully accept that stress is Internally produced. Now, are you going to take Responsibility and do something about it?

Sometimes people will fully recognize that their stress is produced internally, but not take responsibility for creating a change. Part of the reason this happens may be due to the success of Sigmund Freud, who taught that the mind was a wild, woolly, and untrustworthy place, best explored only with professional assistance and "curable" only with a great deal of time and effort.

Certainly there are people who do require professional care, but the large majority of those struggling with daily stress could take care of themselves effectively if they knew how. ActivInsight gives you a way to do this that is as mainstream and stigma-free as going to the gym. So if you're ready to take complete Responsibility for your emotional well-being under any circumstances, up the SPIRAL you go.

That brings us to the *A*, which stands for ActivInsight. Taking responsibility means doing a worksheet—not just thinking of the negation in your head, but actually going through all seven steps on paper (or using the online version I'll describe later) so you have the deepest insight possible. This is the biggest leap up the SPIRAL, the step that moves you out of anger, anxiety, sadness, or victimhood to honesty and greater understanding. You write down the thoughts that you experience as stressful, and then challenge them one step at a time. Just like going to the gym, simply thinking about it does nothing. You have to sweat.

The last step in SPIRAL is the *L* for Leverage. This means that you approach your situation from a higher plane. In some tangible way, you use the insight as leverage to create change in your life from a wiser perspective. Maybe you have an honest conversation, or you write a letter, or apologize, or clarify, or brainstorm, or commit to next steps. ActivInsight is not about remaining on the mountaintop. You take time out to have an insight, then come back down, roll up your sleeves, and make a difference on the ground.

That's the ActivInsight SPIRAL. For any challenge that comes up, if you are angry, frustrated, or depressed, then you're at the bottom (STRESS). If you are able to address the situation calmly and take action, then you're at the top (LEVERAGE). Spiraling up from the bottom to the top involves asking yourself a series of questions to unlock your resistance and then doing a worksheet to get things flowing again.

So where on the ActivInsight SPIRAL would you place yourself regarding the angry person in your life that we're working on? You've experienced Stress. Do you Prefer being right ("She shouldn't get so angry. This is her problem, not mine")? You can go on being right about her, but the price is your own happiness.

If you're ready to move toward peace, can you see that all the stress you experience is Internally produced, or are you still blaming your emotional state on the angry person's outbursts? Blaming is easy to do because as a culture we point the finger at those who violate our standards of acceptable behavior, saying that angry people should manage their anger better. I'm not excusing them, but I'm asking you to see that, whatever the angry person may say or do, his or her anger doesn't produce stress in your life. *Your thoughts about that anger* produce stress in your life. Anger produces noise and other physical sensations, but the emotional reaction you have comes from your own beliefs about what that anger means. This is the only way that emotions can arise. You are like an island without a bridge. Things "out there" aren't able to magically cross over and affect you. Stress arises from your own beliefs.

If you can truly accept that your own thought patterns are the source of your emotions, then it opens the door to Responsibility. You become responsible for your emotional well-being no matter what takes place around you. From this more responsible perspective you may begin to see how the anger of your boss, spouse, parent, or child, just like a traffic jam, is an effect of prior causes. But for most people anger pushes a bigger button because it seems like something the angry person should be able to control. It seems like a moral failure on their part, and it also feels directed much more personally at you than a traffic jam would ever be. After all, traffic jams don't take place in your living room or the middle of your office. But just as with traffic, there is a deeper logic at work, and seeing it can help you find peace. So without in any way condoning the behavior of the angry person in your life, let's see how ActivInsight can shift your perspective and give you greater Leverage.

Think about someone you know who gets very angry. If you can't think of someone in your life right now, find someone who used to get angry at you and write the worksheet from the past. We're going to work on the statement "They shouldn't get so angry."

A QUICK GRAMMAR NOTE: Throughout the book, I generally use the word *they* instead of *he* or *she* to refer to individuals because it makes the worksheets more accommodating. *They* can apply to a man, a woman, or multiple people with minimal mental acrobatics on your part. You're always welcome to personalize the statement on your own worksheet so that it reads, "She shouldn't get so angry," "Tom shouldn't get so angry," "My colleagues shouldn't get so angry," etc.

Fill out the lines of Step 1.

1 Write a concise, complete sentence describing something that you experience as stressful. It's helpful to use the words "should" or "shouldn't." (Ex.: "They should listen to me.")

> *They shouldn't get so angry.*

_____

_____

Then in Step 2, how strongly do you feel this belief to be true? Remember, you want to put yourself in the time and place when you most strongly believed it, then circle the number that feels right to you.

2 How strongly do you feel this belief to be true?

0   1   2   3   4   5   6   7   8   9   10

——————————▶ stronger

Next, how do you feel when you think to yourself, "They shouldn't get so angry"? Do you feel angry yourself? Helpless? Resentful? Tense? Circle the feelings in Step 3a that arise for you with this thought. Breathe while you're doing this. When we confront strong feelings, we sometimes stop breathing, but continuing to breathe as you do the worksheet will help you stay more focused.

3a How do you *feel* when you believe this?
(Circle below or add your own.)

afraid   abandoned   angry   annoyed   anxious

confused   depressed   desperate   embarrassed

frustrated   helpless   hopeless   hurt   impatient

inadequate   insecure   invisible   jealous   nervous

rejected   resentful   tense   upset   worried

When you're doing this step, try to circle at least three of these, but more is encouraged if they strike you as true, and you can always write in additional emotions by hand.

Once you've circled three or more feelings, ask yourself, how do you act when you feel this way? What do you do? Again, the words on the worksheet in 3b are meant to serve as a springboard for your own insights. When this person or group gets angry at you and you feel resentful, for example, do you withdraw, or do you fight back? Do you contemplate walking out, or taking revenge, or doing something to make them feel guilty? Do you eat, or smoke, or drink? Look for the effects of this thought and its related feelings on your behavior, and circle the actions that ring true for you.

3b How do you *act* when you feel this way?
(Circle below or add your own.)

argue   belittle   blame   bully   complain   cry   drink

eat   escape   fight   find fault with   give up   gossip

insult   interrupt   lose sleep   manipulate   obsess

overwork   pity myself   preach   pretend   procrastinate

shop   shut down   smoke   suffer   withdraw   yell

After you've identified your behaviors, take a minute to visually connect the belief in Step 1 with the feelings in Step 3a and the behaviors in 3b. You want to see clearly that it's *not* their anger that makes you complain, cry, withdraw, fight back, or whatever else it is you do. It's your belief that they shouldn't get angry that leads to these feelings and actions. This is an important connection to make. When they're angry, their face gets red, they say certain things, and they do certain things. This is all a reflection of what *they* are thinking. *Your* reactions are a reflection of what *you* are thinking. They have their contracted beliefs, you have yours, and typically these bounce back and forth between you in an argument. To get leverage and change this, you first have to challenge your own beliefs so that the whole equation shifts inside you.

You do this through the negation. So in Step 4, negate the statement you're working on. What's the negation for "They shouldn't get so angry"? The correct answer is:

4 Write the negation of your statement from Step 1. In most cases, you also add "In reality" at the beginning and "at this time" or "at that time" at the end.

> *In reality, they should get so angry at this time.*

_____

_____

Write this on your worksheet.

Then, in Step 5, why is it true in reality that they should get so angry at this time? To help you see this more easily, let's take a brief detour.

Imagine that you're a scientist monitoring a dormant volcano. Miles beneath the volcano's summit, a large pool of molten rock bubbles in a subterranean chamber, trapping gases that slowly build up pressure. When the pressure is high enough, these gases will eventually explode toward the surface opening, throwing magma and ash into the air. But for this particular volcano, that hasn't happened in several thousand years.

And yet, as a scientist you notice changes taking place. Over a period of months, earthquakes occur more frequently deep underground, and infrared satellite imagery shows a change in the volcano's heat activity. These changes intensify, until eventually, with a blast of ash and sulfurous smoke, the volcano erupts. The people living near the volcano are traumatized and say to the media, "This is a terrible thing. The volcano shouldn't have erupted." But you saw the changes taking place. You saw the seismic activity increasing. The argument that it "shouldn't" have erupted is a denial of the laws of physical science and could be made only by someone overlooking the facts. The truth is that, in reality, the volcano *should* have erupted at that time. Its eruption had nothing to do with whether or not people wanted it to erupt. It was simply cause and effect. When people don't see these causes, they often think the effect shouldn't have happened, and they experience stress. But the causes were still there, and seeing them leads to greater understanding and the ability to act or get on with life more easily.

Now let's return to your worksheet, and I want you to use the same objectivity to see why this person in your life, just like a volcano, *should* have erupted at this time. Keep in mind, as always, that you're not saying that you condone their anger, and you're not saying you want it to occur again in the future. You're just learning to see why it happened at this particular moment, because the stress that you're experiencing doesn't come from their anger, it comes from your beliefs about their anger. So why *should* they get so angry in reality at this moment?

Be a scientist. Push yourself to come up with as much proof as you can for why they should get so angry at this time, write it down, and then proceed to the next paragraph.

If you couldn't come up with proof on your own, don't worry. This often occurs when someone starts doing ActivInsight—everything makes perfect sense, but when you try proving a negation on your own, your mind goes blank. This happens because stress results from a blind spot in your awareness, and Step 5 asks you to peer into the blind spot. Almost everybody has trouble at the start, but I haven't met anyone who doesn't get the hang of this after some guidance and practice.

The following proof is drawn from the worksheet of Linda, a physician's assistant, on her boss, Dr. V, who regularly screamed at his employees at the hospital, even in front of patients. When she began this worksheet, Linda was ready to quit. "He shouldn't get so angry" was at least a 10. When she thought about this, she felt tense, exhausted, and abused, which led her to shut down emotionally, work with the bare minimum of effort, and bad-mouth Dr. V to others. Then she got to Step 5 and tried to see why, in reality, he should get so angry at this time.

The first thing that came to her mind was, "In reality, he should get so angry at this time because he's an asshole." That may seem like proof, but profanity and character judgments are always signs to dig a little deeper. So Linda pushed further, and this is what she came up with:

---

5 Write below all the proof you can find that supports the negation being true in reality at this time (or in the past). Don't rush. Be thorough, using an additional sheet of paper if necessary.

> *In reality, he should get so angry at this time because he believes that I did something wrong and that this affects him negatively.*

> *In reality, he should get so angry at this time because he's never learned how to address his underlying beliefs about people's behaviors.*

> *In reality, he should get so angry at this time because he had role models who taught him that anger is an acceptable way of reacting to a situation.*

> *In reality, he should get so angry at this time because his anger is tolerated culturally.*

> *In reality, he should get so angry at this time because he often gets what he wants when he's angry (it works for him).*

> *In reality, he should get so angry at this time because he's not fully aware of how angry he becomes and how this affects others.*

> *In reality, he should get so angry at this time because when he's gotten angry in the past, I've withdrawn, fought back, or complied, none of which helps him learn a better way.*

Do you see how much more thorough this is than Linda's first thought? This was a real attempt to see why this man *should* get so angry at this time. And the last proof was Linda's attempt to see how her own part, however small, might have played into his getting angry at this time.

As a result of her deep reflections on the negation, a change took place. When Linda started the worksheet, she believed Dr. V lacked compassion, empathy, and morals. But after spending time in Step 5, she saw how in reality he just lacked a certain kind of education. This doesn't justify his anger or excuse it, but to Linda, at least, it helped explain it. For the first time since working with him, Linda felt like Dr. V wasn't an insurmountable problem. She saw him as a little boy who had simply never learned a better way to interact with people. And this led to a profound change in how she felt about her job, which I'll share in a moment.

Taking Linda's honesty as a guide, review the list of proof above in Step 5 and see how much of it applies to your situation. Can you come up with any more proof for why, in reality, they should get so angry at this time? Spend a few minutes reflecting on it. Instead of seeing the angry person in your life as a tyrant, see him as you would a child throwing a temper tantrum—unable to express his emotions another way. Just because this person may not be a child doesn't mean that he has any greater skill in this area. We all have areas of weakness.

Then, when you can see this, take a deep breath, look over the list below, and circle the emotions you feel.

6a How do you *feel* when you see the truth of the negation? (Circle below or add your own.)

calm   clear   compassionate   connected   curious
enlightened   enthusiastic   excited   free   grateful
honest   humble   intimate   light   loving   optimistic
peaceful   playful   relaxed   relieved   serene
supportive   tolerant   truthful   understanding

Next, in 6b, how do you act when you feel this way? Can you have a conversation with the other person? Or write them a note? Look for the action steps you can take, and circle or write in what you find.

6b What *actions* might come from this?
(Circle below or add your own.)

accept   apologize   approach   be honest   breathe

clarify   communicate   contribute   delegate   exercise

explore   focus   follow through   forgive   give thanks

listen   make amends   network   open up   participate

prioritize   reach out   share   speak up   support

The final step of the worksheet, Step 7, is to re-rate the belief. With your vision grounded in reality, when you consider their cultural conditioning, their past experience dealing (or not dealing) with their underlying beliefs, their sense of being threatened or negatively affected, and whatever part your own actions might have played, how true does it seem that they shouldn't get so angry at this time? Circle the number that feels right to you.

7 Read your original statement again. How strongly do you feel this belief to be true now?

0   1   2   3   4   5   6   7   8   9   10

weaker ⟵━━━━━━━

Hopefully you went down a few more points on this worksheet than the last one. Each time you do ActivInsight, the steps should become a little clearer, and the proof you come up with should sink in a little deeper. It's a good idea to come back to these early topics after you've done others. Even though you'll still be going through the same steps, you'll find yourself experiencing them differently. The more points you drop on this particular worksheet, the less angry you'll get in the face of other people's anger, and that makes you better able to help them.

In Linda's case, once she no longer believed that Dr. V shouldn't get so angry, she had a talk with him to discuss how his communication style affected her and his other colleagues. She asked for his input on what was going wrong, and thought of ways to improve staff training so that people made fewer mistakes. She also scheduled regular feedback sessions between Dr. V and the staff so that everyone communicated better. In terms of the SPIRAL, that's what Leverage is all about. The point of doing ActivInsight isn't just to feel better. Have an insight, clear your head, then create change.

Now, what if you're the person who gets angry? What should Dr. V do? What I *wouldn't* do is a worksheet on "I shouldn't get so angry." This may be useful in cases where your issue is overwhelming self-judgment regarding anger, but for most people a much better first worksheet would focus on the things that make you angry. For example, "Linda shouldn't make careless mistakes," or "My staff should know what to do by now." Find the specific things that seem to trigger you, convert them to "should" or "shouldn't" statements, and do worksheets on those beliefs. This will help you drill down to what actually provokes your anger, the magma inside the volcano. The more worksheets you do on these beliefs, the less angry you'll become. When you take away the magma, the volcano is just a mountain.

We've now seen ActivInsight applied to the beliefs "I shouldn't be here," "There shouldn't be so much traffic," and "They shouldn't get so angry." Take a break, and when you come back, we're going to tackle a belief that has destroyed relationships, crippled leadership teams, divided families, and even sparked wars. Next up: "They should see it my way."

CHAPTER 6

The Myth of Conflict Resolution

Who in your life should see things the way you do? Your boss? Your coworkers? Your parents? The kids? Somewhere in your life, there is a person or group whom you don't see eye to eye with. That's who we're going to work on next.

You might be thinking, "I don't need to work on this—*they* do. They're the ones who have to have an insight." They might very well benefit from having an insight, but what about the frustration that *you're* feeling? Where's that coming from? I'll give you a hint: It's not coming from them. Remember the *I* in SPIRAL? Maybe someday they'll challenge their beliefs and emerge transformed, but in the meantime, you're the one who is annoyed, so you're the one this chapter is written for. You're going to learn how to eliminate conflict in *your* life, no matter what anyone else may do.

That might sound absurd. In order for conflict resolution to take place, don't both sides have to participate? No, because the real conflict isn't between two divergent points of view. The conflict that you feel is between your belief of how things "should" be and how they really are. When two people each have this internal conflict, it can seem like the issue takes place between them. But this is merely a secondary effect, an echo. The primary conflict takes place inside each person individually. Attempting to resolve the inner conflict by addressing the outer one first is like putting out a basement fire through a top floor window. There may be a better way.

So get out a worksheet, and let's take a closer look at the person in your life you don't agree with. The statement we're going to work on is "They should see it my way." You can personalize it to your situation ("Jan should see it my way," "My coworkers should see it my way," etc.), but write your statement now on the lines of Step 1.

---

1 Write a concise, complete sentence describing something that you experience as stressful. It's helpful to use the words "should" or "shouldn't." (Ex.: "They should listen to me.")

> *They should see it my way.*

_____

_____

Next, rate it. From the most contracted part of yourself, the part that considers them stubborn, foolish, and (let's be honest) just plain wrong, what number would you give it? Circle the number that feels right to you.

2 How strongly do you feel this belief to be true?

0   1   2   3   4   5   6   7   8   9   10

———————————————▶ stronger

Then, in Step 3, when you think, "They should see it my way," how do you feel? Angry? Hurt? Impatient? Circle at least three feelings, writing in any that aren't listed.

3a How do you *feel* when you believe this?
(Circle below or add your own.)

afraid   abandoned   angry   annoyed   anxious

confused   depressed   desperate   embarrassed

frustrated   helpless   hopeless   hurt   impatient

inadequate   insecure   invisible   jealous   nervous

rejected   resentful   tense   upset   worried

Next, when you feel the way you just indicated, how do you act? Some people go on the attack. Others pull away and withdraw. In the corporate world, this belief can lead to "silos" where entire divisions don't talk to one another. In families, it can lead to years of estrangement. How does the belief "They should see it my way" play itself out in your life? Mentally take a step back from yourself and see how you act toward them and others, and circle the relevant behaviors in Step 3b. You can also write in words that aren't listed. Every word in this section has been circled by one person or another for this particular topic, so make sure to consider them all:

3b How do you *act* when you feel this way?
(Circle below or add your own.)

argue   belittle   blame   bully   complain   cry   drink

eat   escape   fight   find fault with   give up   gossip

insult   interrupt   lose sleep   manipulate   obsess

overwork   pity myself   preach   pretend   procrastinate

shop   shut down   smoke   suffer   withdraw   yell

When you've completed Step 3, go on to Step 4. What's the negation for "They should see it my way"?

The correct negation is "In reality, they should not see it my way at this time." So write that on your worksheet:

4 Write the negation of your statement from Step 1. In most cases, you also add "In reality" at the beginning and "at this time" or "at that time" at the end.

> *In reality, they should not see it my way at this time.*

_____

_____

If this seems backward, that's a good sign. It means that you've put your finger on the part of your mind that is contracted and producing stress. The next step is to release the contraction by looking at your thoughts more closely and seeing if they may not be as true as you believed. We do this by focusing on the negation instead of the original belief because challenging the original belief can seem too threatening.

For example, you believe that they should see it your way. I could ask you, "How is that belief false?" This would be a full frontal assault on your belief and one of the most direct routes to insight. But for most people it would be *too* direct and would result in their defenses going up. Our beliefs are ours because we believe them to be true, and jumping so quickly from true to false takes rare flexibility. So instead we ease into this, validating the belief in the first three steps. Then in Step 4 we flip the belief and, instead of proving it false, we prove its negation true. This takes us to the same place ultimately, but instead of knocking down the front door, we sneak in the back.

So instead of telling me how "They should see it my way" is false, tell me how it's true in reality that they should *not* see it your way at this moment. Take a few minutes to see what you can come up with. Don't just keep reading. Push yourself a little. Then continue and I'll suggest some additional proof.

Here are some suggestions for why, in reality, they should not see it your way at this time. These are drawn primarily from two clients—a management team that had been butting heads with one another for months, and a wife, Shannon, who was fighting with her husband, Steve, about their children's education, but they apply to a broad range of conflicts. Reflect on whether or not they apply to your situation. If so, add them to your worksheet.

In reality, they should not see it my way at this time because they have a different set of experiences, leading to a different perspective.

The management committee mentioned above consisted of twenty directors in charge of global decision making for a multinational corporation. They had been arguing for months over their areas of responsibility and the team's strategic direction. Some companies do team-building exercises to overcome these differences, but these exercises generally fail to change the underlying beliefs that keep people apart. When this group gathered for a biannual meeting, we identified their underlying beliefs in order to address the problem at its source. After they got to this step, the committee members realized that part of why the negation was true was that they came from different countries and cultures, so they all had different experiences and perspectives.

The same was true of the married couple. Shannon believed in public school education for kids because it was free and their local charter school was highly regarded. Her husband, Steve, wanted the kids to go to private school, where he felt they would get more attention. "We've had different life experiences regarding education," Shannon said, "so he shouldn't see it my way at this time. I get that. I still think that he's wrong, though." Fair enough. I asked her if *he* might think *she* was wrong. She nodded. That leads to the next proof.

In reality, they should not see it my way at this time because they sincerely think that they're right and I'm wrong.

If someone in a disagreement recognizes that he's wrong, the disagreement is over. But in Shannon's case, Steve thought that he was right and that *she* was wrong. The same was true for the management team members, all of whom felt that their colleagues were mistaken and needed to see the light. Reflect on your own situation. Does the person or people you're working on think that they're right and you're wrong? If so, that's part of why they should not see it your way at this time, and you have to add that to your worksheet. Then consider the next suggestion.

In reality, they should not see it my way at this time because they have different values and priorities than I do. (Specify how.)

In the case of the management committee, some of the members prioritized local or regional issues, while others were more focused on global concerns. Shannon and Steve also had a difference in priorities involving cost, status, and educational opportunities. It can be very helpful to have a conversation establishing common ground, but when you're still experiencing anger or frustration, that conversation is premature. First comes insight, so you can see why the other party *shouldn't* see things your way. Then, when you no longer feel emotionally contracted, you can begin a dialogue. But the way to get there is through proving the negation as thoroughly as you can. Do you see that part of why they should not agree with you at this time is because they have different values and priorities than you do? If so, add that to your worksheet, specifying what these are, and then continue.

In reality, they should not see it my way at this time because they believe that would have negative consequences. (Specify what.)

Again, try to be specific. Shannon was in favor of public school, but Steve thought it might affect their kids' chances of getting into certain colleges. So she wrote that on her worksheet. One member of the management committee felt that his idea for policy change was essential, but everyone else thought it would cause great confusion. So that went on his worksheet. What does the person or group you have in mind think would happen if they did things your way? That's what you want to write down. This can be hard to do, because you think you're right and they're mistaken. But remember the *P* from the SPIRAL. Do you Prefer being right, or being at peace? If you want peace, you have to put aside your desire to be right and build a bridge between your mind and the facts of reality surrounding it. Look over the proof again and put some effort into specifying what they think might happen if they adopted your point of view. Even if you believe you're right, you can learn to respect the intelligence behind their position.

In reality, they should not see it my way at this time because they think that if *I* saw things *their* way, everyone would be better off. (Specify how.)

Do your colleagues think that their way would increase revenues, cut costs, or save time? Does your partner or family member believe that his or her approach would lead to greater prosperity, preserve social values, or cause less harm? What's behind their position? Think about it, and write it down. Specify exactly how they believe their position would improve things.

In reality, they should not see it my way at this time because people they trust are reinforcing their views. (Specify who.)

When our minds are contracted, we tend to think in terms of us versus them. We imagine that *we* have infinite support from friends and family but that those who disagree with us are crazy isolationists living in backwaters of ignorance and denial. Stretch a little bit to see this isn't true. Each person on the management committee who had been fighting for his view had allies in the home offices who reinforced his position. Shannon and Steve could both name friends who agreed deeply with them. This holds true for the person you're working on as well. Other people in his or her life see things the same way, whether they're clergy, doctors, business leaders, teammates, mentors, or simply like-minded friends, and those people are another factor in why the person you're in conflict with should not see it your way in reality at this time. Reflect on this and write it down, and if you can, say specifically who this might be.

In reality, they should not see it my way at this time because I've been wrong in the past, and they may question my discernment. (Specify when.)

This suggestion invites you, as Dudley said, to get really real. Think of any relevant times *when you were wrong,* especially if they thought you were wrong and told you so in advance. So if you made a bad business decision or a poor relationship choice and now you're making another decision in a similar area, your past record is being held against you. Even if you're right now, that past record is part of why they should not see it your way at this time.

It can be hard at first to remember when you've been wrong. Your mind may want to defend itself, saying that you've been right many more times, or they've been wrong even more often than you have. But that's not what you're looking for in this step. You have to push yourself here to see into the slightly obscure parts of your memory that you wouldn't normally pay attention to. When did you make a mistake that they could be aware of? If you can come up with examples, write them down. And if you really can't come up with any, you might ask someone else for help. Other people often remember our mistakes much better than we do. But don't rush this one. The business leaders and Shannon needed some time with this, but they all eventually found examples of when their past opinions or suggestions had proved unwise. Are you fallible? See if you can find when and where.

In reality, they should not see it my way at this time because I could be wrong now. (Specify how.)

That last proof opened you up to exploring this one. If it's possible that you're wrong now, recognize that. Put it in writing. It doesn't mean that you *are* wrong. But if there's even a possibility, acknowledge that as part of why they might not see things your way in this moment. "I guess I *could* be wrong about this," Shannon said. "Maybe it is a safer bet to send them to private school. Maybe the money is justified and they would get a better education, or make more friends, or have some other advantage. I haven't ever really considered that I could be wrong, but I might be."

The management committee members had a harder time with this one at first. People tend to get ahead in business because they're good at being right and they don't second-guess themselves. But the reality is that not everyone in that room was going to be right. The only way that they could all listen to one another and evaluate every option fairly was if each person became open to the possibility of being wrong. As they wrote down ways in which this was possible, the battle lines they had drawn began to disappear.

In reality, they should not see it my way at this time because they have a right to their own opinion.

You may want them to see things your way, you may think they would be better off, but if they have the right to see things through their own eyes, that's worth recognizing. In the case of the management committee, they recognized that they each had the same level of authority, and they were all intelligent, seasoned leaders. Shannon recognized that her husband was a fellow stakeholder in their children's lives. In your case, it may be that the person you're working on is mistaken, but has a right to take a position different from yours. Take a moment to think about whether this could be true, and if so, add it to your worksheet, then proceed to the final suggestion below.

In reality, they should not see it my way at this time because instead of listening to their side and having a calm exchange of perspectives, I've polarized our relationship by attacking or with-

drawing, and this makes their seeing things my way at this time almost impossible, even if I am right. (Specify what you do.)

This is a long one, but it's essential. When you're working on someone else, you always end Step 5 by looking at your part. In this case, you want to see how you may have polarized the relationship by insisting that your way was right. Even if you *are* right, this kind of behavior pushes people away from seeing your point of view and tends to make them adhere to their own perspective even more strongly. Polarization doesn't happen only through dramatic outbursts. A few of the committee members, for instance, had made their feelings known directly, but most had escalated matters through bickering, gossip, and subtle backstabbing. Shannon had become aloof and avoided talking to her husband. Polarization takes many forms. Think about how this proof may apply in your case. And if you can be specific about what you've done (from saying unkind things to suing someone), write that down as well.

The last part of Step 5 is humbling. It's a confession to yourself. Seeing your own part clearly can be difficult, but it pays off enormously in transforming your experience of a situation. Make sure you've spent time coming up with all the proof you can for the negation, then read it out loud to yourself. Here's what we came up with:

5 Write below all the proof you can find that supports the negation being true in reality at this time (or in the past). Don't rush. Be thorough, using an additional sheet of paper if necessary.

> *In reality, they should not see it my way at this time because they have a different set of experiences, leading to a different perspective.*

> *In reality, they should not see it my way at this time because they sincerely think they're right and I'm wrong.*

> *In reality, they should not see it my way at this time because they have different values and priorities than I do. (Specify how.)*

> *In reality, they should not see it my way at this time because they believe that seeing things my way has negative consequences. (Specify what.)*

> *In reality, they should not see it my way at this time because they think that if I saw things their way, everyone would be better off. (Specify how.)*

> *In reality, they should not see it my way at this time because people they trust are reinforcing their views. (Specify who.)*

> *In reality, they should not see it my way at this time because I've been wrong in the past, and they may question my discernment. (Specify when.)*

> *In reality, they should not see it my way at this time because I could be wrong now. (Specify how.)*

> *In reality, they should not see it my way at this time because they have a right to their own opinion.*

> *In reality, they should not see it my way at this time because instead of listening to their side and having a calm exchange of perspectives, I've polarized our relationship by attacking or withdrawing, and this makes their seeing things my way at this time almost impossible, even if I am right. (Specify what you do.)*

After taking this in and seeing the truth of it, how do you feel? "Humble," Shannon said. "I was angry before, but now I'm not angry. I'm more open to figuring out what the best move is for the kids." She circled *humble* on her worksheet and wrote in *open*. "I also feel open and compassionate toward Steve. He really wants what's best for them, and I can see that his position makes sense in his mind."

The management committee members also felt a change. "I feel more connected," one of them said, "as well as enthusiastic and understanding. Before this, I really felt like we were all at odds with one another and were just pretending to be a team. But for the first time I feel like we really are a team, or could be. Our differences make sense. We have a lot to work through and discuss, but we can do that now. It feels very different, like the blocks have been removed."

Look over the list and see how you feel. More understanding? More compassionate? What comes up for you? If you feel just a little of something, you can write "A little" above the words, but try to find three feelings below or add your own.

6a How do you *feel* when you see the truth of the negation? (Circle below or add your own.)

calm   clear   compassionate   connected   curious

enlightened   enthusiastic   excited   free   grateful

honest   humble   intimate   light   loving   optimistic

peaceful   playful   relaxed   relieved   serene

supportive   tolerant   truthful   understanding

Next, when you're feeling the way you just noted, how might you act? What could you do differently? The management committee set aside meeting time to hear out one another's opinions and take a vote. They also established clear areas of responsibility and outlined how decisions would get made for different regions going forward. ActivInsight is never just about feeling better. It helps you eliminate confusion and take action more intelligently. It gives you a simple path to greater communication, respect, and accountability.

Shannon looked over her worksheet at Step 6 and said, "I'm going to have a conversation with Steve, apologize for how stubborn I've been, hear his side, and do more research into the options available. But that's not all. Now that I see this differently, I feel totally different." She smiled. "I'm going home to make out with my husband."

Insight can move us in many ways. See what you come up with.

6b What *actions* might come from this? (Circle below or add your own.)

accept   apologize   approach   be honest   breathe
clarify   communicate   contribute   delegate   exercise
explore   focus   follow through   forgive   give thanks
listen   make amends   network   open up   participate
prioritize   reach out   share   speak up   support

Finally, in Step 7, now that you've seen that in reality they should *not* see it your way just at this time, how strongly would you rate the original belief? What number would you circle if you were being as honest as you could be? Close your eyes, take a few deep breaths, and find the number that feels right to you.

7 Read your original statement again. How strongly do
you feel this belief to be true now?

0 1 2 3 4 5 6 7 8 9 10

weaker ←————————

In this final step, the committee members ranged from 1 to 5. Shannon was a 2. Typically, the more time and effort you spend in Step 5, the more of a point drop you see in Step 7. When this happens, you can feel a release of energy, as if something that had been locked up has become free to move. It can be helpful to do something physical—go for a walk or run, or work out at the gym. Reviewing your worksheet later in the day is also a good idea and can help you integrate this insight more deeply.

It's always a good idea to put your action steps from Step 6 into motion sooner rather than later. And if you do have a dialogue with the other person or group, it's helpful to reread your worksheet to yourself just before you meet. At first, these exchanges can feel a little awkward, and you might start by admitting that you are uncomfortable, saying something like, "Listen, this is a little awkward for me, and I'm not used to expressing myself this way, but I wanted you to know that . . ." Then take it from there.

I've done this worksheet with couples on the brink of separating and have seen it bring them back together as better listeners and more intimate partners. I've also done this with business leaders at for-profit and not-for-profit organizations, helping them strengthen their teams in a much deeper way than ropes courses and typical team-building exercises. Conflict may seem normal in relationships and in business—in some cases it's even considered a sign of passion—but in reality it's always wasted energy. When you have an insight into why someone else should not see things your way at this time, you recover that energy and can use it to improve communications and brainstorm solutions together.

As more people work through the belief "They should see it my way," the nature of how we understand conflict changes. You think *x*, I think *y*. We disagree. But we don't necessarily have a conflict. Conflict takes place when one party thinks the other party's opinion isn't just different—it's *wrong*. Insight helps you see that, much to your surprise, the other person is actually right, *in his or her mind*. This change from conflict to disagreement isn't just semantic. It reflects a real change. You may already be feeling a difference in how you see the situation on which you did this worksheet.

Essentially, what happens with ActivInsight is that you learn to lose. Initially this sounds terrible, because you think that winning is what makes you successful and happy in life. And if you can win, go right ahead. But whenever you experience frustration, anger, or other negative emotions, you've already lost in the sense that you're no longer in contact with the real world and you don't realize it. How many relationships have ended bitterly because individuals were unwilling to see their part in a disagreement? How many businesses have lost enormous talent, money, and experience because both sides of an internal argument were determined to win?

Knowing how to lose doesn't mean that you *want* to lose going forward. It means that when you do lose, you can recover quickly. Everyone loses sometime, but those who don't know *how* to lose will continue to dig themselves in deeper and drag others down with them. Those who do know how to lose, on the other hand, are able to quickly see their mistake and take full responsibility for this, making things easier for themselves and others.

That's what the committee members above learned. Before

doing a worksheet, they had fragmented into silos, each believing the others were wrong and wondering why working together was so unproductive. But really they weren't working *together*. They were working separately at the same time. After doing this worksheet, that began to change. The same was true of Shannon and Steve. He wasn't even in the room, but through insight, their marriage got stronger. As I said earlier, it takes only one person to end a conflict.

Of course, not everything changes in a day. It's a process. But this worksheet broke the ice and got things flowing again. How would the committee members or Shannon know when it was time to do another worksheet? The same way you would—when you experience stress. Stress tells you that, somewhere in your mind, you've lost touch with the world you live in. You then do a worksheet to reconnect your mind to the real world, make any necessary amends, and get back in the game. Do this quickly, but thoroughly. This is not about a rushed apology—you want to really own the lesson. You may want to review this worksheet again to let it sink in deeper. Learning to lose takes some practice, but leads to great gains in the bigger picture.

In the next chapter we're going to take on a slightly more challenging topic. So far we've focused on external challenges in your life. But what if the person you have a problem with is yourself? And what if the problem isn't something you need to accept, like traffic or other people's behavior, but something that you need to actually change? For example, what if you should weigh less? How would you handle that with ActivInsight? In the next chapter, I'll show you.

CHAPTER 7

The Myth of Weight Loss

We all know how to lose weight: First, you have to *truly* admit to yourself that you should weigh less. Then you have to exercise more, eat less, and avoid cheating. Piece of cake. Well, not cake—piece of carrot.

This simple strategy forms the backbone of hundreds of weight loss programs serving millions of people and generating billions of dollars in revenue, yet according to peer-reviewed studies, it rarely works. Instead, what happens in almost every case is that you truly admit to yourself that you should weigh less, you start a program, and you lose a few pounds (fighting hard not to eat the many things you're avoiding). Then you get stressed-out by something, you cheat, and you gain back most of the weight you lost, and in some cases all of the weight plus interest. Many people repeat this over and over, cursing their lack of willpower, telling themselves more forcefully that they should weigh less, and wondering how something as easy as putting food in their mouths could be so hard. This was certainly the experience of Kim, whose story you'll read in this chapter.

To break the cycle, I'd like to make a radical suggestion. What would happen if you questioned the statement "I should weigh less"? Kim knew exactly what would happen. "If I no longer believed I should weigh less," she said, "I would eat everything I want and get even fatter." You may think something similar. But are you so sure about this? Let's go through this worksheet and see how having an insight can help you approach your body and your food choices from a more intelligent place.

First, in Step 1, write, "I should weigh less."

1 Write a concise, complete sentence describing something that you experience as stressful. It's helpful to use the words "should" or "shouldn't." (Ex.: "They should listen to me.")

> I should weigh less.

Next, rate it. Imagine yourself at the beach or getting undressed in front of someone very critical. That's the place you write this worksheet from mentally, because for most of us that's the place we're in when we feel bad about our bodies. How strongly do you feel that you should weigh less?

2 How strongly do you feel this belief to be true?

0   1   2   3   4   5   6   7   8   9   10

⟶ stronger

In Step 3, when you think this thought, how do you feel? Depressed? Embarrassed? Upset? Find at least three feelings of your own, and take your time. This worksheet will be seen by only you, so be as honest as you can.

3a How do you *feel* when you believe this?
(Circle below or add your own.)

afraid   abandoned   angry   annoyed   anxious

confused   depressed   desperate   embarrassed

frustrated   helpless   hopeless   hurt   impatient

inadequate   insecure   invisible   jealous   nervous

rejected   resentful   tense   upset   worried

Now, feeling the way you just wrote down, how do you act? What do you do? We're not looking for positive behaviors such as "I join a gym and try to lose weight." We're looking for the negative behaviors, because those are the ones we'd like to change. Is that when you reach for the bag of chips, the cookies, or the beer? Do you try to hide your body? How do you act socially around new people? How do you dress? What happens to your dating life, or your sex life?

Take a few deep breaths and spend some time looking at all the ways this thought—"I should weigh less"—plays itself out in your actions. For many people, there are dozens of ways this affects their behavior. Find at least three, but if you can find more, circle them, write them in, and use additional paper if necessary. Be thorough.

3b How do you **act** when you feel this way?
(Circle below or add your own.)

argue   belittle   blame   bully   complain   cry   drink

eat   escape   fight   find fault with   give up   gossip

insult   interrupt   lose sleep   manipulate   obsess

overwork   pity myself   preach   pretend   procrastinate

shop   shut down   smoke   suffer   withdraw   yell

Now what's the negation for "I should weigh less"? Write it on the lines of Step 4.

4 Write the negation of your statement from Step 1. In most cases, you also add "In reality" at the beginning and "at this time" or "at that time" at the end.

> *In reality, I should not weigh less at this time.*

_____

_____

For people who have spent a lifetime believing they should weigh less, this negation can seem insane, even traitorous, as if writing it—and worse, *believing* it—will guarantee that you're never going to lose weight. But this worksheet has nothing to do with what's going to happen in the future, at least not in the way you might think. We're not talking about tomorrow. We're not talking about the rest of your life. We're just looking at the facts in this moment. In Step 5, why is it true in reality that you should not weigh less *at this time*?

Be compassionate as you do this step. For example, "In reality, I should not weigh less at this time because I'm worthless" is not a valid piece of evidence. "In reality, I should not weigh less at this time because I sometimes believe that I'm worthless, and when I do, I overeat" *would* be valid (and you could do a separate worksheet later on "I'm worthless" and see what you find). Come up with as much evidence as you can, then move on to the suggestions I'll provide below. Keep breathing.

Here is some possible proof for why, in reality, you should not weigh less at this time. Take time to think about the suggestions below and add them to your worksheet if they strike you as true in your case.

In reality, I should not weigh less at this time because I eat more than my body needs.

This is another good example of starting with the obvious. Those "healthy" bars that you munch on to keep you going, those high-fiber fat-free muffins, and that small handful of candy (repeated multiple times) all add up. If you eat more than you need, either at one time or through repeated snacking, this would be a factor in why you should not weigh less at this time. This isn't about feeling shame. We're going to shift how you relate to your body. But you have to do this for yourself by getting as honest as you can.

In reality, I should not weigh less at this time because I do not exercise daily.

Studies show that daily exercise (even if it's just brisk walking) makes the greatest difference in your weight. If you don't exercise daily for at least thirty minutes, then that's part of why, in reality, you should not weigh less at this time. If you do exercise daily, good for you. We're just getting started with our proof.

In reality, I should not weigh less at this time because I eat for taste (or cost, convenience, etc.), not nutrition.

For millions of years, up until about ten thousand years ago, our ancestors ate mostly meat and whatever fruits and vegetables they could find. There was no candy. There was no pasta. And amazingly, in what surely must have been an evolutionary oversight, there was no pizza.

For many people, the foods we eat today are connected to fond memories of our childhood and our culture. They give us a sense of pleasure we don't want to live without. I understand this because I worked in a bakery, and I know the joys of a homemade sourdough boule. But if you eat a lot of processed foods, especially foods that are high in glycemic load (GL), part of why you should not weigh less at this time is because you eat for taste rather than nutrition. There's no right or wrong here, but there is cause and effect. If that's how you've been approaching food so far, it goes on your list as proof.

You may think that you just can't survive without eating these foods daily, but most people find that a few days after eliminating high-GL foods, they no longer crave them. After a few weeks, new habits take hold, and eating a more nutrient-rich diet is as easy as pie. Well, maybe not pie. Easy as salad.

In reality, I should not weigh less at this time because I am over the age of thirty.

People tend to gain weight as they age, partly from being sedentary (see proof number 2 above), and partly from the effects of aging on the body. If you are more than thirty years old and think you should still weigh the same as when you were a teenager, you're mistaken. For that matter, if you're in your twenties and think you should still weigh the same as when you were a teenager, you're also mistaken. There may be a few people for whom this doesn't hold true, but they are in the minority. Healthy human bodies typically fill out as they get older, especially female bodies. Which brings us to our next proof . . .

In reality, I should not weigh less at this time because I am a woman, and my body is designed to store calories.

Obviously if you're a man, you're going to skip this one. But, women, your bodies evolved to store a certain amount of additional weight as fat so that when you were pregnant or needed to nurse during a famine or food shortage, you could still meet your child's nutritional needs. Millions of years of evolution aren't going to disappear because a few fashion editors like a slimmer cut. Your thighs, no matter how much you hate them, were the salvation of our race's past, and are the guarantors of its future. The more people who recognize the female body for the miraculous life-support system that it is, the sooner these editors will start celebrating bodies as they actually appear. In the meantime, part of why you should not weigh less right now is because you're a woman, and your body didn't read the memo that fat is undesirable because it was too busy keeping the human race alive.

In reality, I should not weigh less at this time because my hormones may not be balanced.

Hormone imbalance used to be fairly rare, but it's on the rise for both men and women. The ubiquity of birth-control pills, the increase in hormone disrupters from plastic and other chemicals in our environment, and the long hours we work stressing our adrenal glands are all factors in our hormone health. This topic goes beyond the scope of this book (I recommend Broda Barnes's book,

Hypothyroidism: The Unsuspected Illness, as a place to start, as well as James L. Wilson's *Adrenal Fatigue: The 21st Century Stress Syndrome*), but it may be part of why you should not weigh less at this time. If that's a possibility, it's worth writing down on your worksheet and learning more about.

In reality, I should not weigh less at this time because when I'm frustrated, upset, or bored, I eat.

Find people who have never been overweight and ask them how they eat. Some of them will say that they eat breakfast, lunch, and dinner, with no snacking and no sense of a connection between their emotions and food. Find people who are trying to lose weight and ask them the same question, and you're likely to hear a different story. When you feel frustrated, upset, or bored, get out a worksheet and break through the issue bothering you. If you've been turning to food instead, then this is part of why you should not weigh less at this time, and it goes on your worksheet.

In reality, I should not weigh less at this time because I restrain myself and then, when something stressful happens, I binge.

Does this sound familiar? You decide you want to lose some weight, so you avoid certain foods. No dessert. No carbs. No candy. You feel great about what you're giving up, even though it seems like you're abandoning your children. But you're not going to think about that, because you have willpower and determination. That is, you have willpower and determination until a crisis arises, and then it's peanut M&M's to the rescue. How could you have tried to deny them?

Why does this happen? According to researchers like Daniel M. Wegner, Janet Polivy, and C. Peter Herman, the millions of dieters today trying not to think of their beloved foods actually invest these items with even greater desirability, and as a result inevitably give in and overeat them. By restraining yourself, you're almost guaranteeing that you're going to binge when something breaks your resolve (such as alcohol or stress). This doesn't refer to people who simply stop eating certain foods without a care. Restraint refers to people who desire something intensely but attempt to deny it, building up subconscious pressure toward fulfillment.

To understand restraint, it's helpful to think of this in terms of a *stress threshold,* which is the amount of emotional turmoil you can endure before a change in your behavior takes place. Terms like "the boiling point" and "the final straw" point to this, suggesting that what's affecting you are external pressures. But, in actuality, your stress threshold reflects internal beliefs. When enough of these beliefs are in play, you may get angry (like Dr. V), do drugs (like the men at Phoenix House), or eat. We all have a particular behavior we employ when we reach our threshold.

One reason dieting fails is because when you tell yourself you have to avoid eating certain foods, that very act of restraint pushes you toward your threshold. This is part of why most weight loss attempts set people up to fail. From the very beginning, you're telling yourself that there's something wrong with you, and the stress that you experience as a result of that belief pushes you toward your threshold. Just saying, "I should weigh less," produces guilt that makes you want to eat.

So how do you lose weight, then? Daily exercise and the gradual adoption of better food choices without harsh restraint can help. ActivInsight can also help, because it gives you a tool to take apart issues as they arise so that you don't cross your threshold and go running into the arms of a hot fudge sundae. You can't easily change the behaviors you give in to when you cross your threshold, but you can keep yourself from getting there by regularly working through the challenges in your life. Work on your mother, your father, your partner, your boss, your job. These may seem unrelated to your weight loss goals, but your mouth is part of your head. Keep your head clear and the challenge of slowly adopting new eating habits is much more manageable. And if this hasn't been your approach so far, if you've been trying to lose weight through restraint and willpower, then this is part of why you should not weigh less at this time, and you would write that down.

In reality, I should not weigh less at this time because when I eat something "bad," I figure I might as well give up and start again tomorrow.

Drs. Polivy and Herman call this the "what the hell" effect, as in, "Now that I've already messed up, what the hell, I might as well pig out." Of course, this makes absolutely no sense. Your body doesn't give you a free pass because you've eaten one forbidden thing. It responds to every calorie. But if you've thought and acted this way in the past, you're far from alone. And that "what the hell" thinking would be part of why you should not weigh less at this time, so it goes on your worksheet.

In reality, I should not weigh less at this time because I am genetically programmed to weigh this much.

You may have noticed that losing a few pounds is manageable, but losing more weight gets progressively harder. This is because your body has a genetically predetermined range within which it functions optimally, called a set-point range.

Set-point ranges are part of our evolutionary heritage. Our ancestors lived in regions where food periodically became scarce, and their bodies developed the ability to keep weight on in spite of limited resources. Today, with food available everywhere in the West, this same caloric thriftiness is no longer as useful, but your genes don't know that. So part of why you should not weigh less at this time may very well be because you're genetically built to store whatever calories you consume. If this seems true in your case, add it to your worksheet.

You can lower your set-point range with daily exercise. Dieting also affects your set point, but not the way you might think. See the next proof for details.

In reality, I should not weigh less at this time because I have dieted in the past and raised my set point.

Dieting shifts your set-point range, but *the wrong way.* When you diet, you force your body to meet its nutritional and energy needs with fewer calories than it requires. Basically, you starve yourself. Your body at first loses weight, then alters its metabolism so that it conserves energy more efficiently during the apparent famine. This is when you plateau and wonder why you're not losing weight anymore. Soon hunger kicks in, because your body is telling you to gain back the weight it needs to function optimally. But, taking this as a challenge to your willpower, you ignore this. And so your body adjusts so that if and when you do stop starving, it will prepare itself even better for a famine in the future. That's right, dieting *raises* your set point, so that when you eventually end your diet and start eating again, your body gains *more* weight than it had before.

This is why people who have spent years yo-yo dieting generally end up at a higher body weight than they were before they started. They have, in effect, taught their bodies to prepare for larger and larger famines. If that sounds familiar to you, this goes on your worksheet. (And if you want to lower your set-point range, again, consider daily exercise.)

In reality, I should not weigh less at this time because I'm actually healthier at this weight.

This one is a little harder to grasp because it challenges something many people have never questioned—that they need to lose weight or they'll live unhealthier lives and die at a younger age. For most people, this simply isn't true. Consider the following three facts:

1. It has never been proven that obesity itself causes heart disease (or atherosclerosis). In analyzing autopsy results of more than twenty-three thousand people in fourteen different countries, the International Atherosclerosis Project found no association between body weight and atherosclerosis. And some studies have shown that heavy people have *healthier* arteries than their skinny peers.

2. One of the broadest studies ever conducted on the relationship between diet, body weight, and human health is the famous Seven Countries Study begun by Ancel Keys in the 1950s and still going on. In observing more than ten thousand men in Finland, Italy, Greece, Japan, the Netherlands, the United States, and the former Yugoslavia, the researchers concluded that *high body weight is unrelated to morbidity.* In fact, it was the *thinnest* people who died soonest, not the fattest. The study reported that:

   > long-term survival showed no relationship throughout the distribution of body weight, except for the excess risk of being in the *lowest* class of body mass. Moreover, survival was *greater* in those who gained weight in middle age than in those who did not gain or who lost weight. [Italics added.]

3. Dr. Steven Blair of the Cooper Clinic in Dallas has studied the health and fitness of more than twenty-five thousand people over a twenty-year period. His findings? Again, thin

people who were unfit died twice as often as obese people who were fit. According to Dr. Blair, "Many people classified as obese by current standards actually have a good health profile. You are better off being fit and having a fat waist than having a small waist and being unfit."

Dozens of other studies have supported the conclusion that being overweight is not harmful in and of itself, and that it's the sedentary lifestyle and poor eating habits that often go with being overweight that are the problem. For those who exercise (just thirty minutes a day of brisk walking, for example) and eat properly, *body weight is not harmful.* In some studies, it even appears to offer a protective effect.

Why, then, do so many doctors and nutritionists continue to tell their patients to lose weight for better health? Health care professionals have been taught to follow a standardized height-weight table or Body Mass Index as their reference. These tables, popularized in the early 1940s, were an attempt to convert MetLife life insurance data into an easy-to-read prescriptive format: if you were this tall, you should weigh this much in order to maximize your longevity. This format is very easy for your doctor to use.

But the data that these tables came from were not so neat. Sometimes thin people lived shorter lives, and obese people lived longer. To keep things simple, MetLife created a fictional linear relationship where there wasn't one. Going strictly by the original data, many people would live longer and healthier lives if they *gained* weight, not lost it. And people who would technically be considered obese today actually have the greatest chance of living the longest lives.

But most doctors haven't seen the original data. They have been trained with a cleaned-up version that distorts the relationship between body weight and life span, so the misinformation continues.

The bottom line is that in the most extensive long-term studies, the people most likely to die younger are those who are *too skinny,* not those who are too fat. The *very* obese do have special health concerns, but this is a tiny minority of the population. The extra weight that the majority of us carry—even if it's 25 to 35 percent above the so-called ideal for your height—is not in itself harmful if you exercise regularly and eat smart. In short, fat can be fit. You might do some research into this to prove it to yourself. Books like *The Diet Myth,* by Paul Campos, *Breaking the Diet Habit,* by Janet Polivy and Peter Herman, and *The Dieter's Dilemma,* by pioneers William Bennett and Joel Gurin, can be eye-opening reading. And if you realize that part of why you should not weigh less at this time is because you may be healthier at this weight, add it to your worksheet.

Of course, some people have known all along that there's nothing wrong with being larger than average. And that brings us to my last suggestion.

In reality, I should not weigh less at this time because part of me knows that my body is okay as it is.

You may have spent years believing that thinner is better, but not everyone shares this limitation. A growing wave of people celebrates diversity not just in race, sexual identity, and other variables, but in size as well. African-American and Latino cultures as a rule don't subscribe to the same waiflike ideals as white culture (especially white metropolitan culture). And before the concept of fat as unhealthy was created, white people didn't subscribe to this, either. The fact is that, in spite of pressures from the media, many people can still see beauty at any size. If you can find that in yourself, you should write that on your list. And if someone in your life, like your partner, thinks that you are beautiful as you are, you would write that down, too, because that's another part of why your body is okay as it is, and why you should not weigh less at this time.

So here's the proof listed together. Take time to read it out loud.

---

5 Write below all the proof you can find that supports the negation being true in reality at this time (or in the past). Don't rush. Be thorough, using an additional sheet of paper if necessary.

> *In reality, I should not weigh less at this time because I eat more than my body needs.*

> *In reality, I should not weigh less at this time because I do not exercise daily.*

> *In reality, I should not weigh less at this time because I eat for taste (or cost, convenience, etc.), not nutrition.*

> *In reality, I should not weigh less at this time because I am over the age of thirty.*

> *In reality, I should not weigh less at this time because I am a woman, and my body is designed to store calories.*

> *In reality, I should not weigh less at this time because my hormones may not be balanced.*

> *In reality, I should not weigh less at this time because when I'm frustrated, upset, or bored, I eat.*

> *In reality, I should not weigh less at this time because I restrain myself and then, when something stressful happens, I binge.*

> *In reality, I should not weigh less at this time because when I eat something "bad," I figure I might as well give up and start again tomorrow.*

> *In reality, I should not weigh less at this time because I am genetically programmed to weigh this much (my set point).*

> *In reality, I should not weigh less at this time because I have dieted in the past and raised my set point.*

> *In reality, I should not weigh less at this time because I'm actually healthier at this weight.*

> *In reality, I should not weigh less at this time because part of me knows that my body is okay as it is.*

Can you come up with any more proof? It's important that you don't move to Step 6 until you get a sense of the negation being true at a single point in time. This doesn't mean that you're never going to weigh less. It just means that you shouldn't weigh less *right now.* What happens when you see this honestly, without self-criticism?

When Kim first did this worksheet several years ago, she had been telling herself for decades that she should weigh less. She had tried dieting, exercise, national weight loss programs, and even three months of phentermine, a controversial appetite suppressant prescribed by her doctor. While each of these provided positive short-term results, Kim would always gain the weight back and feel like a failure.

She heard of ActivInsight through a friend and gave it a try. In Step 2, Kim rated this belief a 10. In Step 3, this belief made her feel frustrated, guilty, inadequate, insecure, and demoralized, and that led to her complaining, obsessing, withdrawing, and avoiding social situations. When she wrote down "In reality, I should not weigh less at this time" in Step 4, it seemed like treason. But as she went through Step 5, something happened.

"It was surprising," Kim said, remembering her first experience:

Somehow seeing the truth of my situation did exactly the opposite of what I thought it would do. It left me with no emotional self-abuse at all. Not even a little. It was like an emotional weight was lifted, and I could just see the truth. I ate too many empty calories, I didn't exercise enough, I didn't follow the program, I ate out of frustration. Seeing it all so logically like that, I ended up feeling a great sense of clarity and awareness, and I was motivated to make changes. I felt excited to follow through and find support, and it totally changed my outlook on my body and my weight goals. I became more confident. My husband even noticed the change, and he ended up doing ActivInsight on a problem that was bothering him at work. (And he's not normally into self-help.)

I'll share more of Kim's story in a moment, but when you can clearly see that in reality you should not weigh less at this time, what do you feel? Do you feel a sense of clarity as well? See what comes up for you, and write it in Step 6a.

6a How do you *feel* when you see the truth of the negation? (Circle below or add your own.)

calm   clear   compassionate   connected   curious

enlightened   enthusiastic   excited   free   grateful

honest   humble   intimate   light   loving   optimistic

peaceful   playful   relaxed   relieved   serene

supportive   tolerant   truthful   understanding

Next, when you feel this way, how might you act? When people believe that they should weigh less, they tend to beat themselves up and eat (high-GL) comfort foods. But when they can see that they should *not* weigh less *at this time,* that results in a sense of lightness, and they can go for a walk or eat more intelligently. This is the Paradox of Insight: *it's the negation that helps you achieve what you want to achieve, not the original stressful belief.* You'll see this repeatedly as you complete other worksheets in this book.

When you see clearly that you should not weigh less at this time—not tomorrow, not forever, just right now—how do you feel? See what feels right to you, and circle it on your worksheet.

6b What *actions* might come from this? (Circle below or add your own.)

accept	apologize	approach	be honest	breathe
clarify	communicate	contribute	delegate	exercise
explore	focus	follow through	forgive	give thanks
listen	make amends	network	open up	participate
prioritize	reach out	share	speak up	support

Finally, how would you rate this belief now, "I should weigh less"? When you started, it probably rated 10. How true is this statement in reality now?

7 Read your original statement again. How strongly do you feel this belief to be true now?

0   1   2   3   4   5   6   7   8   9   10

weaker ⟵————————

How did you do? If you took your time and reflected on each of the steps as we went along, this was a real workout. But in this workout, you don't try to lose physical weight—you lose mental weight. This may be even more important, because while many studies show that heavier physical weight alone doesn't harm you, the heavier mental weight in your life most certainly does. It's the mental weight that brings on your depression, resentment, shame, and self-criticism, affecting how you feel, how you act, and how you eat. The mental weight also triggers stress hormones that make your body more likely to store fat.

The more mental weight you lose by working on issues in your life—not just your body, but your relationships, your job, and anything else—the lighter your head becomes. And, as Kim relates below, this puts you in a very different position.

After working on "I should weigh less," I worked on other issues, including my parents. They died when I was young, and the belief that they shouldn't have died had always been a heavy burden for me, affecting me in many ways, including how I eat. Doing a worksheet on that thought completely changed how I saw what happened. It was really a big insight. Four years later, the insight is still clear. I'm typically more of a right-brain thinker than a logical one, but ActivInsight gave me a process that helped me comfortably use logic to dispel my worries and anxieties. I've applied it to a number of issues over the last few years. And do I weigh less today? Yes! I always strive for better, but I have a plan that works and a state of mind that can support that plan, which makes it so much easier.

The myth of weight loss claims that in order to lose weight you have to first feel bad about your appearance, and that the best motivator is self-criticism. But in my experience, peace of mind is a much more powerful fuel. Keep doing worksheets on the things that bother you—and learn more about the realities of weight loss—and you may find taking care of your body much easier. That makes sticking to any program far more sustainable.

But it's not enough to just think of doing worksheets. Schedule them on your calendar, recruit friends to help, and make it a habit to take out your frustrations with a pen, not a fork. The more you do this, the less stress you'll experience, and the more in control you'll feel about which foods you eat. When your mind is clear, you can make smart choices, exercise daily, and feel good about yourself, not just in the future, but as you are right now. And that's having your cake and eating it, too. That's right, I said cake. Enjoy.

CHAPTER 8

The Myth
of Success

Success means different things to different people. In the business world, it may mean a more prestigious title and greater income, or it could be a function of your company's performance. In the not-for-profit world, success is often tied to fund-raising or how many lives you've helped improve. Students define success with grades and other measures of academic achievement. For athletes and coaches, it's a function of wins. For actors, success is based on ratings and reviews. For parents, success may simply be raising healthy children with good values.

However you define success, you may believe that you should have achieved more of it by now. I'm sure you can think of people you know, people who may not be as talented as you are, who somehow have achieved greater success than you in some area (income, happiness, work/life balance, parenting, etc.). "*I* should be more successful," you tell yourself. You're not alone. Right now, that thought is on the minds of countless people stewing in frustration at their desks, ordering another drink at their local bars, or lying in bed and staring at the ceiling.

But wait. Isn't the thought "I should be more successful" a motivator? Yes, it is. It's motivating people to drink, smoke, lose sleep, overeat, fight, and feel miserable about themselves. Contrary to popular belief, it's *not* motivating the kind of behavior you desire.

To make this clear, let me return briefly to the topic of the last chapter, "I should weigh less." There are people on this Earth who simply eat when they're hungry, stop when they're full, and go on with their lives. They have no angst over their bodies, and they spend no time regretting what they see in the mirror. They don't even own a scale. The thought "I should weigh less" doesn't cross their minds. It's not that they've come to accept themselves, because that suggests a process of transcendence. There was nothing to transcend. They simply never believed that there was anything about their weight to be concerned about; it's a total nonissue.

Now what would happen if these people took it upon themselves to improve their fitness? They would learn what they needed to learn and start doing it. No resistance, no drama. Set a goal, and take steps toward it.

This may sound far-fetched, but there are people in your life who live this way now. Healthy living is not an obsession to them; it's just something they do. Or maybe you know people who are loving, attentive parents. They don't beat themselves up thinking, "I should be a better parent." They simply understand what it takes to be the parents they want to be, and they do it. You know people who work hard at school or at the office because they have their sights set on performing well. They don't agonize over the belief "I should be more successful." They're too busy making it happen.

I'm pointing this out to help you challenge the idea that without stress we become unmotivated. The truth is that without stress, we learn faster and we sustain our level of interest longer. We're in the zone. Athletes know this. They try reaching a state of flow where the contracted, stressed-out mind disappears and all that's left is the impersonal sense of intelligence in motion. But you don't get to this impersonal, effortless zone by struggling. You get there by eliminating the sense of struggle, and that takes place through insight.

So now we're going to apply ActivInsight to the topic of success. When you get to Step 5, I'll share the story of a financial advisor named Sam who deeply believed that he should be more successful. But first, I want you to start the worksheet on your own. It doesn't matter whether you define success in terms of money, your career, family time, or something else. Whatever success means to you, if you think you should have more of it, hold this in mind, then write on the lines of Step 1 of your worksheet:

1 Write a concise, complete sentence describing something that you experience as stressful. It's helpful to use the words "should" or "shouldn't." (Ex.: "They should listen to me.")

> *I should be more successful.*

_____

_____

Then in Step 2, rate how strongly you feel this belief to be true. Remember that you want to do this from your most concentrated feeling. Think of people who you believe are more successful than you are, and then bring to mind the success you think you should have achieved as well. From that place, how strongly would you rate this belief?

2 How strongly do you feel this belief to be true?

0   1   2   3   4   5   6   7   8   9   10

———————————➤ stronger

Keep the intensity of your thoughts and feelings high as you go through the worksheet. In Step 3, when you think "I should be more successful," what feelings come on the heels of that thought? Circle or write them in below.

3a How do you *feel* when you believe this?
(Circle below or add your own.)

afraid   abandoned   angry   annoyed   anxious

confused   depressed   desperate   embarrassed

frustrated   helpless   hopeless   hurt   impatient

inadequate   insecure   invisible   jealous   nervous

rejected   resentful   tense   upset   worried

And in Step 3b, when you feel this way, how do you act? What do you do? Do you beat yourself up? Do you resent people who you think are more successful than you are but shouldn't be, or those who seem to stand in your way? Do you cheat or cut corners? Do you lose sleep? Take time to review how this thought expresses itself in your life.

3b How do you *act* when you feel this way?
(Circle below or add your own.)

argue   belittle   blame   bully   complain   cry   drink

eat   escape   fight   find fault with   give up   gossip

insult   interrupt   lose sleep   manipulate   obsess

overwork   pity myself   preach   pretend   procrastinate

shop   shut down   smoke   suffer   withdraw   yell

Next, what is the negation for "I should be more successful"?
Write it on the lines of Step 4. The correct negation is below:

4 Write the negation of your statement from Step 1. In
most cases, you also add "In reality" at the beginning
and "at this time" or "at that time" at the end.

> *In reality, I should not be more successful at this time.*

_____

_____

Some people don't like writing down this negation, but at this
point, having done several worksheets, you may be feeling a sense
of recognition because you're already starting to see how it's true. If
so, that's a good sign that you're getting the hang of ActivInsight.
Now go to Step 5, where, with as much compassion for yourself
as you can muster, you prove why the negated statement is true.

Compassion is always an important part of this step, but it's especially important when you're working on self-statements. As you come up with proof, you don't want to write something like "In reality, I should not be more successful at this time because I'm a loser." As I mentioned in the chapter on anger, any time strong words of criticism for yourself or someone else appear on your worksheet, drill down to uncover what those words are referring to. If you think you're a loser, for example, what does that mean? Did you make key mistakes that derailed your goals? Then you would write, "In reality, I should not be more successful at this time because I made several key mistakes and am still learning how to succeed." The worksheet is never about blaming yourself or others. It's a vehicle to see through blame to the underlying truth.

Take a few minutes to come up with as much proof as you can, looking first at the external circumstances and then at yourself (again, with compassion). Write this on your worksheet before proceeding. Throughout this book, if you skip right to my suggestions, you won't get nearly as much out of this as doing it on your own first, even if you don't come up with much. Just making the effort to find proof opens up your mind in important ways. So look for why you should not be more successful in reality at this time, and then proceed to the next paragraph.

Below are suggestions that can help you see why you should not be more successful at this time. If any of these suggestions rings true for you, add it to your worksheet or a separate sheet of paper. If you think of other pieces of evidence, include those as well.

In reality, I should not be more successful at this time because I don't want to put in more time and energy than I already do.

In some highly competitive fields, the time demands required to achieve success are almost unfathomable. Athletes wake up in the dark to train. Finance professionals are at their desks by five a.m. Some people seem to never go home. You may say you should be more successful, but when it comes to putting in the time, you may want balance in your life even more than you want success. If so, that is part of why you should not be more successful than you are at this time, and it goes on your list. Success is partly a function of time put in, which brings us to our next proof.

In reality, I should not be more successful at this time because I don't use my time and energy as effectively as I might.

Organization, prioritization, delegation, and follow-through are skills that can be raised to an art form, but only through practice. If you have not mastered these arts, then in reality that's part of why you should not be more successful at this time. The more challenging your goal is, the more this matters. This doesn't mean that you can't sleep, take a vacation, or spend time with your family. But you may want to adopt a better system for organizing your time and energy so that your approach is less haphazard. Many of the most successful people have done this. It's not easy, but it's possible. And that leads to the next suggestion for proving this negation.

In reality, I should not be more successful at this time because what I'm trying to achieve is difficult. (Specify how.)

Every day you successfully accomplish things that require intelligence: getting dressed, feeding yourself, walking, driving, carrying on conversations. We take our success at these things for granted (unless we lose the ability to do them), and instead we set our sights on loftier goals. This is perfectly natural, but it shouldn't blind you to the fact that part of why you should *not* be more successful *at this time* is that, in reality, you're trying to do something difficult, whether it's build a business, raise a family, get recognized in a crowded field, or all of the above. After all, if it were easy, you would have done it already. As simple as this is, millions of people overlook it when they stubbornly believe they should be more successful than they are. Reflect on this, and if you can specify on your worksheet exactly how what you're trying to achieve is difficult, write that in as well.

In reality, I should not be more successful at this time because I'm working in a crowded field with talented competition.

No matter how talented and ambitious you are, if you're competing against others who are also talented and ambitious, then this is also part of why you should not be more successful at this time. That could change in the future if the competition falls away or you create a new market, but if it's true today, that's reality. Recognize it by adding it to your worksheet.

In reality, I should not be more successful at this time because I don't want to sacrifice my integrity.

Sometimes we know exactly how to get ahead, but it would mean breaking the law or doing harm in some way. Look at how many people achieve great success and then end up embroiled in scandals or in jail because of the shortcuts they took to get there. Whether it's performance enhancement drugs in sports, shady deals in politics or business, or cheating in school, if you've chosen not to participate in these activities because you want to achieve your success honestly, good for you—but make sure to note that on your worksheet. In reality, part of why you should not be more successful at this time is that you want to earn your success without sacrificing your integrity, even if this means that success will take longer.

In reality, I should not be more successful at this time because part of becoming successful is out of my control. (Specify how.)

You may have a clear goal that you're trying to achieve, but even if you've done everything right, there are factors beyond your control: timing, competition, the marketplace, the economy. It's the presence of these variables that makes success elusive. Stretch your mind to see that there's more to success than just desire and strategy. There are external forces to contend with and circumstances beyond your control. Whatever these are in your case, write them down. Be specific. This isn't intended to excuse your supposed lack of success. It will help you see your situation more clearly.

In reality, I should not be more successful at this time because I haven't reached out enough to others who can help me. (Specify who.)

Success today is a team effort. The days of going it alone and taking all the credit are quickly being replaced by interconnected groups who share the workload and the rewards and who get things done in a fraction of the time. If you're not building a network of relationships to help get you where you want to go, you're probably being outpaced by people who are, and this is a part of why you should not be more successful at this time. So this would go on your worksheet.

Additionally, if you think that it's improper or inappropriate to ask people you know for help, this is also part of why you should not be more successful at this time. You may want to find the belief that's stopping you (such as, "If I ask people for help, they'll think less of me" or "Asking for help is a sign of weakness") and do a separate worksheet on it. As the world continues to shrink through technology, partnering with others is only going to become more crucial to achieving success, and those who go it alone, whether out of stubbornness or fear, will fall further behind. So write down this proof, and then ask yourself, who are the people in your world who know and trust you, and who have advice, experience, or connections that could be helpful to you? Look over your contact list, think about it, and add their names to your worksheet.

In reality, I should not be more successful at this time because I haven't made my goals attractive to other people and their own goals.

Maybe you've made the effort to reach out to others, but when you got their attention, did you talk about *your* goals and what *you* want to achieve? We don't want to hear about you. We want to hear about how it benefits us, and *how our goals can be met through yours.* Then you turn us into allies. So if you've been trying to find success by focusing on what it will do for *you,* you'd want to write down this proof. Start to think about how you can help *us* succeed, and your own success may happen more easily.

Here, then, is the proof all listed together. Read it out loud to yourself with any other proof you can come up with on your own:

---

5 Write below all the proof you can find that supports the negation being true in reality at this time (or in the past). Don't rush. Be thorough, using an additional sheet of paper if necessary.

> *In reality, I should not be more successful at this time because I don't want to put in more time and energy than I already do.*

> *In reality, I should not be more successful at this time because I don't use my time and energy as effectively as I might.*

> *In reality, I should not be more successful at this time because what I'm trying to achieve is difficult. (Specify how.)*

> *In reality, I should not be more successful at this time because I'm working in a crowded field with talented competition.*

> *In reality, I should not be more successful at this time because I don't want to sacrifice my integrity.*

> *In reality, I should not be more successful at this time because part of becoming successful is out of my control. (Specify how.)*

> *In reality, I should not be more successful at this time because I haven't reached out enough to others who can help me. (Specify who.)*

> *In reality, I should not be more successful at this time because I haven't made my goals attractive to other people and their own goals.*

At the beginning of this chapter, I mentioned that you would meet Sam, a financial advisor for a large brokerage firm. Sam has been a top producer at the firm for several years, regularly earning all-expenses-paid reward trips to beautiful resorts with his wife and other top producers. His wife loved these trips, but for the last few years Sam was less than completely thrilled about going. Some of the other advisors had books of clients that were three or four times the size of his book. "I should be more successful," Sam told himself, shaking his head.

In addition to golf, tennis, and sightseeing, the brokerage firm organizes educational breakout sessions for those who want to pick up new skills while on vacation. That's where I met Sam. I was teaching an ActivInsight workshop called Resilience 101, and Sam and his wife attended. His class came up with the proofs above.

"Every one of these proofs is true for me," Sam said. "I don't want to work harder than I do, because I want to spend time with my family. I spend way too much time with small clients and not enough time prospecting for big ones. I could make more money selling products with a higher commission, but I don't want to do that to my clients unless I feel it's right for them. I can go right down the list. But the ones that really get me are the last two. I haven't reached out enough to others who can help me, and I haven't made my goals attractive to them and their goals. I see that. I really see why I should not be more successful at this time. Before going through this, I would have thought that seeing that would depress me, but now I'm fired up to make some changes."

Before doing this worksheet, people always think it's going to be dispiriting or that it will rob them of their motivation, yet afterward, like Sam, they find themselves energized. When you see the truth of the negation and take it in, how do you feel? Clearer? More honest? Identify the feelings that come up for you with your insights, and note them in Step 6a.

6a How do you **feel** when you see the truth of the negation? (Circle below or add your own.)

calm   clear   compassionate   connected   curious
enlightened   enthusiastic   excited   free   grateful
honest   humble   intimate   light   loving   optimistic
peaceful   playful   relaxed   relieved   serene
supportive   tolerant   truthful   understanding

Then, when you feel this way, what might you do? Some people explore time management systems, commit to prioritizing their activities better, or go through their contacts list to see who can be helpful. Sam handed off his smaller clients to another financial advisor in his office and committed himself to focusing only on high-net-worth individuals. He joined a golf club so that he could meet more of these potential clients. And he created referral letters and new marketing materials that let people know how he could help them meet *their* goals. What ideas do you have for ways you can put this insight into action in your life?

6b What **actions** might come from this?
(Circle below or add your own.)

accept   apologize   approach   be honest   breathe

clarify   communicate   contribute   delegate   exercise

explore   focus   follow through   forgive   give thanks

listen   make amends   network   open up   participate

prioritize   reach out   share   speak up   support

Put these action steps on your calendar, and enlist others to hold you accountable over a specified period of time. Remember that we're not negating your goal of achieving success. We're eliminating the friction that prevents you from achieving success in a way that's stress-free and sustainable.

Finally, let's rate the belief we began with: "I should be more successful." Thinking about what you've realized, how true would you rate the original belief at this moment?

7 Read your original statement again. How strongly do you feel this belief to be true now?

0   1   2   3   4   5   6   7   8   9   10

weaker ⟵————————

Congratulations on completing another ActivInsight worksheet. The more points you drop, the more your mental and emotional contractions unwind, and the more energy gets liberated for you to do what you need to do to be more successful in the future.

At this point you may notice something interesting about ActivInsight. Before you have an insight, the original statement seems true and the negation seems false. Then after you have an insight, especially if you drop more than five points, the original statement seems false and the negation seems true, even obvious. So obvious, in fact, that this whole process may seem like nothing more than common sense. "Of course I shouldn't be more successful *right now*," you might say. "That's not telling me anything I didn't know."

But if you gave the original statement anything higher than a 0, it *is* telling you something you didn't know. Like Sam, you thought you should be more successful. You obviously didn't mean you should be more successful *in the future*. You meant *at this time*. But the contracted mind can't see how confused this is. The worksheet helps educate it.

This education happens so naturally through ActivInsight that sometimes we say we knew it all along. It's one of the quirks of real insight that after we experience it, we often deny that it just took place. This is another reason we do this process on paper as opposed to verbally. We're left with tangible proof of the distance we've covered.

One way to cover even more distance is to work on multiple aspects of the same issue. For the topic of success, for example, a related topic is money. If you had more money, you could eliminate your bills, you could get the house you always wanted, you could do things for people you care about, and you could sleep at night not worried about the future. Some things in life aren't certain, but if you had more money, you would definitely be happier. Right? Let's just see about that.

CHAPTER 9

The Myth of Financial Happiness

In this chapter, we're going to explore the relationship between money and happiness.

As you begin, remember that what makes ActivInsight harder for some topics than others isn't the steps involved—these remain the same no matter what you're working on. What makes it harder is the amount of resistance you have to challenging your beliefs. A belief like "There shouldn't be so much traffic" is relatively easy to challenge because, with a little coaching, you can fully admit to yourself that there *should* be so much traffic at this time, for a number of specific reasons. But a belief about money may grip your mind more strongly, and so will require a stronger commitment to seeing the truth. The truth is available—it's present in your own life if you look for it—but you have to be willing to see it. Review the ActivInsight SPIRAL in chapter 5 if this isn't clear to you.

If you are willing to challenge your beliefs, the next step is to write down your thoughts in a concise statement. In most cases, you can do this by "finding the should" in your thought process. It would be perfectly acceptable to write, "I should have more money." Similar to the worksheets you've already completed, that statement would lead to proof clarifying why you have exactly what you have.

You could also phrase the statement in Step 1 as "I need more money." I mentioned earlier that we don't always work on "should" statements. Stressful thoughts take many forms, and beliefs without "shoulds," like "He's a terrible person" and "I'm a failure," are worth investigating if you think they're true. "I hate my job" is another worthy contender, as is "I want them to like me." Different formulations provoke different insights, though some of these (like that last one) can be subtle and usually require a little coaching in order to explore fully.

So how do you decide which way to phrase your belief? You can always use a "should" statement by default. That's what I do, and what I recommend. Most people find the "should" formulation simple, straightforward, and broadly applicable. But there are times when a different phrasing would be even more productive. To help you decide among several choices, I want to introduce something I call *negation-checking*.

Negation-checking involves quickly finding the negation for a statement in your head *before* you do Step 1. This allows you to evaluate how productive the statement you're considering would be for you personally. For example, the negation for "I should have more money"—"In reality, I should not have more money at this time"—prompts you to see why you should not currently have more money than you do. The negation for "I need more money," however—"In reality, I don't need more money at this time"— steers you more toward recognizing your true needs, which is a slightly different insight. We'll work on a "need" statement in chapter 11 so you can feel the difference. But negation-checking gives you a quick preview of where you're headed so you can determine which insight would be most beneficial.

Negation-checking can also prevent you from working on statements that are improperly phrased. For example, let's say that Peter is angry at Paul, and Peter finds himself thinking, "I shouldn't punch Paul. I shouldn't punch Paul." Hearing about this new ActivInsight process, Peter decides to do a worksheet, and writes down for Step 1, "I shouldn't punch Paul," which seems perfectly well-phrased because it's short, it's concise, and it has a "should." But then Peter gets to Step 4 and writes, "In reality, I *should* punch Paul at this time," and then comes up with forty reasons why this is true. So he goes out and beats up Paul, who, understandably, tells everyone he knows that this ActivInsight stuff is not very good.

But what Peter should have worked on was a statement such as, "Paul shouldn't have _____," filling in the blank with whatever he believed Paul shouldn't have done. A quick negation-check of his statement would have helped Peter see that he was going in the wrong direction. ActivInsight never encourages harmful behavior toward yourself or others. If it ever seems to, especially while you're proving the negation, you've misunderstood things somewhere along the line.

Let's use negation-checking now to help phrase the statement for our next worksheet. I want to focus your attention on the relationship between money and happiness. Both the statements "I should have more money" and "I need more money" are phrased properly, but these statements (and their negations) don't address the happiness component. What about "I'd be happier if I had more money"? It's not a "should" statement, but, as I said, not every statement will be, and it does focus on the area we want to explore. It's also a very commonly held stressful belief. What would a negation-check reveal?

The negation for "I'd be happier if I had more money" is "In reality, I would not be happier if I had more money at this time." But now we have a problem. The problem is that this negation is conjectural. Instead of grounding you in the truth, it asks you simply to imagine a different outcome. The same would be true for statements like "I'm going to lose my job" and "Something bad is going to happen," whose negations are "In reality, I'm not going to lose my job" and "In reality, something bad is not going to happen." (We can leave off "at this time" for these because it's implied and would sound awkward.) For both of these negations, you don't know what's going to happen, yet you're being encouraged to imagine that you do. But the point of the negation isn't to use your imagination. The point of the negation is to *stop* using your imagination and see life as it really is.

To remedy this, when you're working on statements involving future or hypothetical conditions, you add "I know that" to the beginning of the sentence. This gives you "I know that I would be happier if I had more money," "I know that I'm going to lose my job," and "I know that something bad is going to happen," which negate to "In reality, I *don't* know that . . ." followed by the rest of the sentence. Can you feel the difference? Now the negation isn't asking you to pretend to know something you don't. Instead, it points to the limits of your knowledge and invites you back to the present moment.

You'll get a better sense of this as we go through the worksheet together. On the lines of Step 1, write the following:

1 Write a concise, complete sentence describing something that you experience as stressful. It's helpful to use the words "should" or "shouldn't." (Ex.: "They should listen to me.")

> *I know that I would be happer if I had more money.*

_____

_____

_____

Then, in Step 2, rate this statement from the place you most believe it:

2 How strongly do you feel this belief to be true?

0   1   2   3   4   5   6   7   8   9   10

———————————▶ stronger

Next, in Step 3, what feelings arise when you think this thought? When you feel sure that you would be happier with more money, but you don't have more money, how do you feel? Anxious? Frustrated? Take a moment to explore this, finding three or more emotions below.

3a How do you *feel* when you believe this?
(Circle below or add your own.)

afraid   abandoned   angry   annoyed   anxious

confused   depressed   desperate   embarrassed

frustrated   helpless   hopeless   hurt   impatient

inadequate   insecure   invisible   jealous   nervous

rejected   resentful   tense   upset   worried

In Step 3b, when you feel this way, what behaviors take place as a result? Do you envy people with more money? Do you begrudge the life you have now? Do you focus on making money as the key to happiness, overlooking other things that could bring you joy? Take time to consider all the ways this belief plays itself out in your behavior, and circle or write in your actions overleaf.

3b How do you *act* when you feel this way?
(Circle below or add your own.)

argue   belittle   blame   bully   complain   cry   drink

eat   escape   fight   find fault with   give up   gossip

insult   interrupt   lose sleep   manipulate   obsess

overwork   pity myself   preach   pretend   procrastinate

shop   shut down   smoke   suffer   withdraw   yell

Pause after Step 3 to look at the cause-and-effect relationship between what you think, how you feel, and how you act. Your emotions and behaviors don't come from your lack of money. They come from your thoughts. Can you see that? Some people claim that money is the root of all evil, but money is just money. Unless you bury it next to a tree, money is not at the root of anything. The thoughts people have about money produce the behaviors we call evil. When these thoughts shift, so do the behaviors. So, let's write the negation. What's the negation for "I know that I would be happier if I had more money"?

The negation for "I know" statements is "I don't know" so the correct answer is, "In reality, I *don't* know that I would be happier if I had more money."

4 Write the negation of your statement from Step 1. In most cases, you also add "In reality" at the beginning and "at this time" or "at that time" at the end.

> *In reality, I don't know that I would be happier if I had more money.*

You're welcome to add "at this time" if it helps you, but can also leave it off for "I know" negations because it's implied.

In Step 5, how is it true that in reality, you *don't* know that you would be happier if you had more money? I realize that you probably believe you *would* be happier, and you could easily come up with proof for that. But Step 5 invites you to explore the flip side of your present belief. Is there any way in which the negation is true from your own experience? The more proof you can find for this negation, the more you decouple the connection in your own mind between money and happiness, and it's that connection that causes stress, not the lack of money. But you need to come up with your own proof to see this. So take a few minutes to see what you can find, then continue with the suggestions below.

Here is some possible proof for Step 5 of your worksheet. Think it over carefully and see if it's applicable in your experience:

In reality, I don't know that I would be happier if I had more money because I know people who have more money than I do who are not happier than I am. (Specify who.)

Think of people you know who have more money than you do: your friend in finance, your rich neighbor, that person you grew up with who inherited a small fortune. Focus not on their houses or cars, but on their sense of happiness. When they lie down at night, are they really happier than you are?

First, your mind will go right to the people who you think *are* happier, but I want you to find the people you know who *don't* seem happier. Take your time and be thorough (you may want to look through your address book). Write down anyone you know who has more money than you do but who doesn't seem happier overall. Then continue to the next proof.

In reality, I don't know that I would be happier if I had more money because I know people who have less money than I do who seem happier than I am. (Specify who.)

This is the flip side of the last proof. Look through your address book again. Do you know anyone who has less money than you do, but who seems to enjoy life more than you? It may be someone who works for you, or a member of the clergy, or someone you've met through a nonprofit you support. Somewhere in your life there is a person who is financially less well off, yet seems to enjoy life more. (In fact, there is an entire class of people like this: children.) Whoever you can find in your life that has less money of his own but is happier goes on your list. Don't rush this. Reflect. Then go on to the next proof.

In reality, I don't know that I would be happier if I had more money because there have been times when I had more money than I do now and I wasn't happier. (Specify when.)

Can you find any time in your past when you had more money than you do now and were not happier? This is challenging because of our tendency to glorify the times when we had more money, especially if we then lost it quickly, but try. If you can find specific episodes from your own life when you had more money but were less happy overall, such as, "When I worked for _____, I made more money but I was miserable," or "When I was married to _____, we had more money but I was less happy," write it down. Then continue.

In reality, I don't know that I would be happier if I had more money because I've had *less* money than I do now and at times was happier. (Specify when.)

Next, find specific evidence from the past when you had *less* money, but were happier than you are now. For example, "I was broke in college, but was in love." Or "I had less money at my first job, but enjoyed what I did." Make sure you're specific and that you write it down, even if you need a separate sheet of paper. You always have to write down these things because you've had proof of the original belief lodged in your head as a result of years of cultural conditioning. Physically writing down your proof helps you see it clearly enough to overturn these assumptions. Be honest, be thorough, then continue.

In reality, I don't know that I would be happier if I had more money because when I think about the things that have brought me the most joy in life, they weren't things that I bought. (Specify what.)

What has brought you the most joy in your life? Many people answer this by mentioning their husband, wife, boyfriend, girlfriend, children, or pet. These relationships aren't fulfilling because of money. They're expressions of love that would be just as rewarding even if money had never existed. For other people, what brought them the most joy was something difficult they achieved, or a passion like music, or a charity they were involved with (and could have been meaningfully involved with even without money).

If you want to be richer, you do need more money. But if you want to be happier, money may not be what you're missing. This proof helps you see that, dissolving the subconscious connection between happiness and material goods. So take your time to think about what has given you the most joy and how those things were not really about money. Write down what you find, then continue.

In reality, I don't know that I would be happier if I had more money because I would most likely get used to the higher level of wealth and take it for granted, as I already have. (Specify when.)

Forget about the future for a moment. How happy are you *right now* with your financial state? You're doing better than some people, but things could definitely be better, right? So how happy would you say you are on a scale from 0 to 10? A 6?

Now look at the material things in your life, and find items that at the time you bought them represented a step up in material wealth: a flat-screen TV, a new computer, a better car, a bigger house or apartment, fancy shoes. At the time of purchase, you were very excited. And then what happened? Eventually you got used to it. And you began thinking that if you could just reach the *next* level of purchasing power, *that* would bring you long-standing happiness. But why would that be any different? You would just be at a 6 then, too.

Consider how much better off Westerners are now than half a century ago. If you could transport people from the past into our homes today, they would assume we must all be royalty. Huge color TVs. Air-conditioning in every room. Phones that fit in our pockets and can be used anywhere. We're living in material goods paradise. But according to polls, we are no happier overall than people were half a century ago.

This is because people tend to adapt to their new circumstances and raise the bar on their desires to an even higher level.

When they do this, they no longer feel as happy with what they have. Look for proof of this in your life. Look for things that you've bought and adapted to, and write them down on your worksheet. Maybe it's a car, or a watch, or a dress. Make sure it's something you bought (not a relationship). You're looking for previously exciting things that you've become accustomed to and now take for granted. This is part of the proof for why in reality you don't know that you would be happier if you had more money. You would probably just adapt again. Find evidence of this from your life, write it on your worksheet, then continue to the last suggestion.

In reality, I don't know that I would be happier if I had more money because extensive studies have shown that more money doesn't equal greater happiness.

You can successfully complete a worksheet like this one just by looking at evidence in your own life, as you've done in the proofs above. But since the relationship between money and happiness has been so widely explored in the social sciences, you can bring this evidence into your worksheet as well.

Social psychologists David Schkade and Daniel Kahneman have spent years exploring the relationship between money and happiness. And they've repeatedly found that, when we are asked to evaluate our own happiness (or someone else's), we do this with a pronounced bias. We focus on a single variable like money or climate, and then make a broad assumption. Schkade and Kahneman call this a *focusing illusion*. It's as if we're focusing on a single picture and assuming that it represents the whole movie. But our sense of happiness in life doesn't come from just one variable. It's drawn from a much larger pool of minute-to-minute experiences.

Here's an example of a focusing illusion. If you ask poor people, "How happy are you?" they will mentally focus on their poverty and say that they're unhappy. If you then ask rich people the same question, they will mentally focus on their wealth and say that they're very happy. But if you then ask both groups to actually measure their sense of happiness at multiple points over the course of the day—as Schkade and Kahneman have done—you will find that, in reality, there is no difference between the two groups. In other words, the rich people aren't *experiencing* greater happiness. They're just *reporting* greater happiness. And they do this because of how their minds focus on certain factors when making an assessment.

An earlier study, and a classic in the field, also provided evidence that more money doesn't equal greater happiness. In the late 1970s, psychologists Philip Brickman, Dan Coates, and Ronnie Janoff-Bulman tracked down twenty-two lottery winners to see if their financial windfalls resulted in greater happiness. These scientists' findings surprised psychologists and laypeople around the world. Not only were the lottery winners *not* happier than people who hadn't won the lottery, but the winners also seemed to take *less* pleasure in the simple things in life after winning.

That was more than thirty years ago, and yet the myth that more money leads to greater happiness still survives. It even gained strength in 2008 when two economists at the University of Pennsylvania, Justin Wolfers and Betsey Stevenson, reexamined several decades of global data on income and well-being and published a report on their findings. Their conclusion? There is a "robust relationship between greater income and greater well-being." Newspapers around the world ran articles on the story.

Figure 1 below illustrates the data that Wolfers and Stevenson published. Each country is represented by a dot. On the horizontal axis, you have how wealthy the citizens in that country are on aver-

Figure 1: Income and Reported Life Satisfaction

Source: Betsey Stevenson and Justin Wolfers, the Wharton School at the University of Pennsylvania

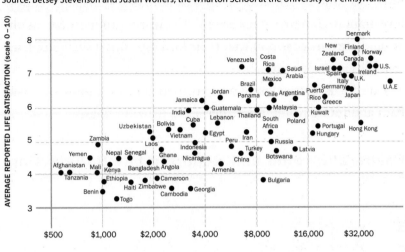

age—GDP per capita. And on the vertical axis, you have how happy the citizens report being on average. So the wealthier a country is, the farther right it appears, and the happier it is, the higher up.

You can see that the happiest country, the one highest up, is Denmark (surprise, Hamlet). The richest, all the way to the right, is the United Arab Emirates (UAE). The poorest country, at the left, is Afghanistan, and the least happy, on the bottom, is Togo. The specific countries shuffle around a bit each year as the survey data change, but the overall distribution remains very similar. Economists would look at this distribution and point out that the trend is that countries with more money correlate with higher self-reported happiness levels. If you were to average the graphic above into a single line, that line would rise from the lower left to the upper right, telling you that as GDP per capita goes up, happiness tends to follow.

Economists see the world in trends. They process enormous amounts of data in order to glean the big picture, and then say

things like "Money does buy happiness after all." This happens
to be the kind of sensationalistic headline that newspaper editors
love—and that newspapers around the world printed when Wolfers and Stevenson announced their findings. But it's still not true,
and I'll show you why.

Let's focus more closely on two particular data points—Costa
Rica and Hong Kong. Here they are isolated in figure 2:

Figure 2: Income and Reported Life Satisfaction
Source: Betsey Stevenson and Justin Wolfers, the Wharton School at the University of Pennsylvania

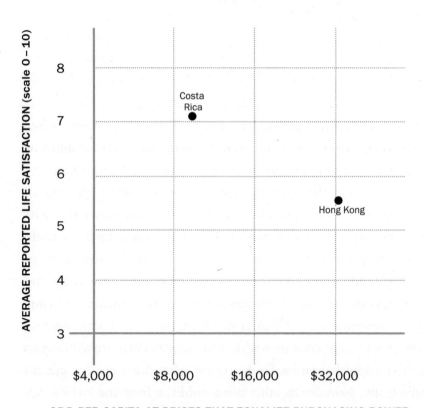

As you can see in figure 2, the average person in Hong Kong
makes more than three times the income of the average Costa

Rican, yet the people in Costa Rica report being significantly happier. So why do economists and newspapers proclaim that "more money equals greater happiness"? What they're reporting on is the trend line, an abstract creation of statistical averaging. But you don't live your life on this abstract level. Your life is lived as one of the dots. And there are dots who experience greater happiness with less money—many of them. You probably listed some from your life on your worksheet already. What you need to know is what actually separates you and them, not what the overall trend is. What makes relatively poor people in Costa Rica say that they're happier than the wealthier people in Hong Kong?

The answer, as you might have guessed, comes down to thoughts. Money cannot make people happy. *Thoughts about money* make people happy. Everything is a function of subconscious beliefs circulated from person to person throughout a culture. The primacy of thought receives no mention in the headlines, but it's undeniable. If a bank accidentally transferred ten million dollars into your account three minutes ago and then fixed the error before you noticed, you wouldn't have experienced a surge in happiness over the past three minutes. Money itself has absolutely no ability to provoke your emotions directly. Only thoughts can do this.

"But," you might ask, "if more money results in thoughts that make people feel happier, couldn't we then say that money makes people feel happier?" No, because this misrepresents the nature of what's taking place. *Certain* thoughts about money make *certain* people happier *for a brief period of time*. But this is a very different statement. Now, we're not talking about money and well-being, we're talking about thoughts and well-being, which brings up the possibility of raising national well-being not just by *in*creasing the amount of money people have, but also by *de*creasing the amount of contracted thoughts.

I'm not suggesting that governments discontinue trying to raise GDP and the standard of living, but I am suggesting that, in addition to changing external conditions, we also focus on changing internal ones. The reason that you may find yourself feeling unhappy when, say, the average Costa Rican might not is because you believe that there shouldn't be so much traffic, or that someone in your life should see things your way, or that you should weigh less. The number of counterfactual beliefs in your head, not the number of figures in your bank account, determines how happy or unhappy you are with your life. Some cultures may circulate fewer of these beliefs, and as a result they enjoy life more. But you don't have to know what your fellow citizens are struggling with in order to increase your own happiness. Simply find the beliefs you have about how life should be different, and challenge them one by one. The more you do this, the more you'll enjoy life. And as greater numbers of people within a country realize this and challenge their limiting beliefs, the country as a whole (or the family, team, organization, etc.) changes as well.

So, coming back to your worksheet, if you can see that part of why you don't know that you would be happier if you had more money is because extensive studies prove that more money doesn't necessarily lead to greater happiness, you would write that down. Seeing this doesn't mean that you give up making money, but it might help you relate to money more clearly. So look over the proof below, read it out loud to yourself, and see how true it feels.

5 Write below all the proof you can find that supports the negation being true in reality at this time (or in the past). Don't rush. Be thorough, using an additional sheet of paper if necessary.

> In reality, I don't know that I would be happier if I had more money because I know people who have more money than I do who are not happier than I am. (Specify who.)

> In reality, I don't know that I would be happier if I had more money because I know people who have less money than I do who seem happier than I am. (Specify who.)

> In reality, I don't know that I would be happier if I had more money because there have been times when I had more money than I do now and I wasn't happier. (Specify when.)

> In reality, I don't know that I would be happier if I had more money because I've had less money than I do now and at times was happier. (Specify when.)

> In reality, I don't know that I would be happier if I had more money because when I think about the things that have brought me the most joy in life, they weren't things that I bought. (Specify what.)

> In reality, I don't know that I would be happier if I had more money because I would most likely get used to the higher level of wealth and take it for granted, as I already have. (Specify when.)

> In reality, I don't know that I would be happier if I had more money because extensive studies have shown that more money doesn't necessarily lead to greater happiness.

What happens when you've done this step sincerely, looking hard at your own life and really thinking about the relationship money has to your happiness? I'll share with you what happened to Chris, a schoolteacher who firmly believed that he would be happier if he had more money.

Chris loved teaching, but he was beating himself up over his financial situation. Then he learned ActivInsight. After doing worksheets on a few other topics to get a sense of how the steps worked, he decided to tackle his beliefs about money. First he did a worksheet on "I should have more money" and found many reasons why, in reality, he should *not* have more money at this time—among them, he didn't have a trust fund, he hadn't won the lottery, he lived in an expensive city, he didn't save his money, and he worked as a schoolteacher making a relatively small salary. He laughed after proving the negation.

"It quickly became obvious that 'I should have more money' was not true," he said. "But I still believed that I'd be happier if I had more money. I could take my girlfriend on a great trip. We could get a bigger place. It would improve my quality of life. I didn't see how another worksheet could make me view that differently, but I was willing to try it anyway."

Looking over his next worksheet, Chris said:

I was able to remember times when I had less money and was really happy, like college. I remembered making *more* money the year before I was a teacher and feeling like my life had no meaning. I have high school classmates who now make a ton of money but are taking antidepressants. The money doesn't seem to be making them happier. And I met kids at an orphanage in Mexico last year who had practically no money but seemed like the happiest kids on Earth. When I look at the real world instead of my beliefs, I can see that money and happiness don't go hand in hand the way I thought. I really don't know that I would be happier if I had more money. And seeing that opened up a space for me, like a cloud was lifted. I feel like I'm more *here*. And I feel good about my life. I love my job.

When you realize that you don't know that you would be happier if you had more money, what feelings come with that realization for you? Circle or write on your worksheet whichever feelings you can identify:

6a How do you *feel* when you see the truth of the negation? (Circle below or add your own.)

calm   clear   compassionate   connected   curious

enlightened   enthusiastic   excited   free   grateful

honest   humble   intimate   light   loving   optimistic

peaceful   playful   relaxed   relieved   serene

supportive   tolerant   truthful   understanding

And when you feel this way, how might you act? What could you do now, or what might you stop doing that you did before? This doesn't mean that you have to stop making money. Chris noted, "If someone gave me a raise, I'd take it. I wish teachers were paid better. But this worksheet helped me stop feeling torn about what I do for a living, so I could commit more to the students. And I've been putting off things like traveling with my girlfriend because I thought I needed more money. But that's not true. We can travel on the cheap. There are lots of ways we can be happy without having more money than we have."

Think about what actions might come up for you from your insights, then circle or write in your responses overleaf.

Finally, look at your original belief again. You know you would be happier if you had more money. In reality, do you know that for a fact? Take a few deep breaths and fill out Step 7.

7 Read your original statement again. How strongly do you feel this belief to be true now?

0   1   2   3   4   5   6   7   8   9   10

weaker ⟵

Good job completing another worksheet. Later in the day, review your worksheet to see if you can add any more proof and deepen your insight further.

Remember that this worksheet isn't telling you not to make money. For most of us today, money is a part of life. It's also not telling you that having more money won't make you feel happy. It certainly can, depending on your beliefs. What this worksheet does tell you is that, if you had more money, sometimes you would be happier and sometimes you would be unhappier, which is to say that your life would be pretty much just like it is now. To improve your net level of happiness, you can try to increase the things that bring you joy (like spending time with loved ones), but it also makes sense to decrease the things that seem to bring you pain. Write down whatever you think is wrong with your life, and challenge these beliefs through ActivInsight.

This is a very different dynamic than positive thinking or motivation. To help you see this more clearly, I want to discuss how ActivInsight compares to some of the other processes you may be familiar with. We're now at the halfway point in the worksheets we're going to do together in this book, and it's a good time for a brief intermission. In the next chapter, instead of doing another worksheet, I want to step back and address how ActivInsight compares to a few other popular techniques in the self-help marketplace. Where will we begin? Here's a hint: it's a secret.

CHAPTER 10

ActivInsight
in Context

No single transformational process is right for everyone and everything, so it makes sense to have a number of tools in your tool kit. If you find that a glass of wine or a workout helps you deal with stress, great. If you're partial to meditation or yoga, terrific. Maybe you just want to vent to a friend, or watch a movie. I've tried all these things and more, and have enjoyed them.

That said, this doesn't mean that every solution we turn to is equally effective. After all, you can pound a nail with the side of a wrench, but a hammer was designed to do the job more efficiently. And among hammers, there are claw hammers, club hammers, sledgehammers, and other hammer varieties you've probably never heard of, each designed to work slightly differently. Many processes try to change how you think, feel, and act, but the differences among these processes are worth understanding. I can't address every tool out there, but I can explore some of the most popular ones, starting with *The Secret*.

In 2006, Rhonda Byrne's viral movie and book became global bestsellers, teaching people "the secret" to greater health, wealth, and happiness. What is the secret? In the words of one of the book's coauthors, the secret is:

Everything that is coming into your life you are attracting into your life. And it's attracted to you by virtue of the images you're holding in your mind. It's what you're thinking. Whatever is going on in your mind you are attracting to you.

This is called "the law of attraction." From the marketing of the book and movie it can seem that this "secret" has been buried for thousands of years, but Jerry and Esther Hicks have been teaching the law of attraction since the late 1980s, and Jane Roberts shared her version of it in the 1960s. Before that, in 1953, Norman Vincent Peale wrote *The Power of Positive Thinking,* a book that remained on the *New York Times* bestseller list for more than three years, sold millions of copies, and served as a motivational touchstone for countless baby boomers. Peale offered similar advice, presented in surprisingly similar language:

This is one of the greatest laws in the universe . . . This great law briefly and simply stated is that if you think in negative terms you will get negative results. If you think in positive terms you will achieve positive results. That is the simple fact which is at the basis of an astonishing law of prosperity and success. In three words: Believe and succeed.

The not-so-secretive thread goes back further still. In 1937, Napoleon Hill wrote *Think and Grow Rich,* which has sold more than fifteen million copies around the world and is one of the bestselling books of all time. According to Hill:

[Our] brains become magnetized with the dominating thoughts which we hold in our minds, and, by means with which no man is familiar, these "magnets" attract to us the forces, the people, the circumstances of life which harmonize with the nature of our dominating thoughts.

Hill repeatedly calls this "the secret" to getting rich. But even he wasn't the first to make these claims. In 1908, William Walker Atkinson stated in *Thought Vibration, or the Law of Attraction in the Thought World:* "I believe that 'thoughts are things,' and that the Law of Attraction in the thought world will draw to one just what he desires or fears."

The law of attraction was a key part of the New Thought movement, a wave of self-help teachers who published hundreds of pamphlets in the late nineteenth and early twentieth centuries. If this "law" is a "secret," it's one that people have been writing about prolifically for more than a hundred years.

I don't fault Ms. Byrne for adding some marketing sizzle to get people's attention. Even if the concept isn't new to everyone, it will be new to those who've never heard of it, and the idea that you can change your life by concentrating on your thoughts obviously resonates for many people over several generations. At first glance, ActivInsight's focus on your underlying beliefs seems to be in the same camp: change your thinking, change your life. So is it?

Not exactly. While I agree with the New Thought movement's premise of our thoughts creating our reality, my own take on how this works is much less mystical and based more on simple psychology. In order to explain what I mean, let's take a closer look at the relationship between your thoughts and your emotions.

When you feel bad, when you're upset or frustrated about something, where is this emotion coming from? What produces it? Over the course of history, different answers have been offered. One of the first, and also one of the most authoritative, came from Aristotle in his *Rhetoric,* where he emphasized the cognitive model of emotions.

According to Aristotle, emotions come from your thoughts. You think something, and you feel the effect of that thought as an emotion. You think about a deadline coming up, for example, and you feel anxious. You think about getting a raise, and you feel excited. Thoughts about snakes or sharks might make you feel frightened. Thoughts about someone you love may result in joy.

We speak as if external things provoke feelings in us directly ("He really makes me angry," "She hurt me terribly"), but with a little reflection most of us can admit that it's our *thoughts* about things that generate our emotions. There's a consistency and logic to this relationship. You can run different thoughts through your mind and watch as the associated feelings arise in your awareness. This is what actors often do to generate emotional performances. They put themselves in a certain place mentally, and feelings result. Clearly, thoughts produce emotions. How could anyone think it works otherwise?

But William James, the brilliant father of modern psychology, had a completely different take on emotions. In the 1880s, James suggested that, first, there's an event in the world, then a physiological reaction to that event, and then, in noticing this reaction, we experience emotions. This was called the James-Lange theory of emotion (Danish physiologist Carl Lange came up with the same theory independently). Here is how James put it:

> Common sense says, we lose our fortune, are sorry and weep; we meet a bear, are frightened and run; we are insulted by a rival, are angry and strike. The hypothesis here to be defended says that this order of sequence is incorrect . . . and that the more rational statement is that we feel sorry because we cry, angry because we strike, afraid because we tremble . . .

According to James, we say we're scared because we are aware of ourselves running away, or we say we're upset because we notice ourselves crying. Admittedly, people often seem to experience feelings without being conscious of an initiating thought. If a big change has just taken place in your life, it can feel like the waves of emotion are coming on their own, without any conscious thought attached. Listening to a piece of music can also seem to take you to a place of emotion beyond thought, as can being physically touched.

But research since James's time, especially the work of Magda Arnold, has proven that emotions are produced *after* thoughts, not before. Emotions don't happen randomly of their own accord. They are surface reflections of deeper mental terrain. The incredible range of emotions that humans experience is testament to the incredible range of this terrain.

Which brings us back to "the secret." When it comes to how you feel, your thoughts *do* create your reality. They create your happiness, your sadness, your frustration, or your sense of boredom, but this doesn't require the universe's magical involvement. You simply think something, and you experience the effect of that thought emotionally. If we had to call it a law, we could call it the cognitive law of emotions: What You Think Is What You Feel. You create your own reality in the sense that your emotional world is a by-product of what's on your mind.

But what about the larger claim that the world around you is also created by your thoughts? Law of attraction supporters propose that the universe is like a pile of iron filings that shape-shift according to your "magnetized" thoughts, or, to use a different metaphor popularized in *The Secret,* the universe is like a genie waiting to grant your every wish if you just focus your mind the right way. I agree that your thoughts *do* create the world around you, but in my experience this, too, is rooted in psychology.

Have you ever noticed that, when you believe someone is arrogant, you dismiss the times he humbly helps others and, instead, you focus like a laser beam on when he seems self-absorbed? If you believe you need to lose weight, when you look in the mirror your eyes will go right to your gut or thighs. On the flip side, when you first fall in love with someone, all you see is how perfect he or she is, even if your friends and family try to suggest otherwise.

You've heard the expression "seeing is believing," but a better way of describing this is "believing is seeing." Your beliefs, whether positive or negative, are like molds that shape the raw input of the world you live in. Psychologists refer to this as a *confirmation bias*. You interpret new information in terms of old preconceptions, confirming what you already knew, even if it's not true. In a very real sense, you don't see things as they are. You see things as you believe them to be.

Believe that things are going great, and everything seems to fall your way. Believe that life is miserable, and the world seems stacked against you. But the universe isn't physically rearranging itself based on your thoughts. You're simply interpreting it differently, because your experience of life is subjective.

This observation has a long history, but Shakespeare probably captured it best in *Hamlet:* ". . . for there is nothing either good or bad, but thinking makes it so." Things simply are. They have no significance on their own. Your interpretations and your resulting emotional experiences are imposed on top of the world through your thoughts. That makes your thoughts pretty powerful. As far as your own experience is concerned, your thoughts really do create the world you're living in. But it's not that you're creating your reality by "manifesting" it. You're just seeing it through the filter of your own beliefs.

So then, why not adopt positive thinking or "the secret"? If your thoughts impose meaning on the world, why not toss out the bad thoughts, repeat to yourself some good ones, and experience a happier life? The problem with this strategy is that your negative thoughts aren't like images in a slide show. You can't just swap them. They may seem to float freely on the surface of your mind, but they're more like buoys, anchored in the deep. And the mechanics of positive thinking fail to address the way in which thoughts are attached.

Let me give you an example to illustrate. Let's say Tanya, who hasn't done ActivInsight, believes the thought, "I should be more successful." When she thinks this, Tanya's mind will come up with images of people who are more successful than she is and ways in which she doesn't quite measure up. And as a result, Tanya will feel miserable. Wanting to feel better, she fills her head with positive images—images of a bigger house, more money, a better job . . . whatever success looks like for her. Then she tries to achieve this success by visualizing it and repeating, "I can do it" (positive thinking), or by living as if it's true and trusting that the universe is already in the process of bringing it to her (law of attraction).

The mind that initiates this movement into positive thinking or attraction believes that it should be more successful. That belief must be in place, or the need to "think positively" or "attract success" wouldn't exist. So the root of this activity, the place it's coming from, is the deeper recognition that whatever success Tanya has right now isn't quite enough. Added on top of that is the new belief, which admittedly feels much better. Remember, What You Think Is What You Feel. Thinking "I should be more successful" feels depressing and dark. Thinking about the success she's going to have, or the success already working its way through the ethers to her, feels much better. But underneath this, the original belief remains.

This is why I call these approaches *additive*. You take the belief that bothers you—about success, your body, your love life, whatever it is—and you *add* to it a new belief. This makes perfect sense, because no one likes feeling bad, and the added belief does feel better. But it's also shortsighted, because you're overlooking the deeper thought buried down below. It's like putting a coat of new paint on rotting wood. It may look better superficially, but the core problem isn't being addressed.

I suspect this is why so many people who engage in positive thinking or invoke the law of attraction feel that their lives are an emotional roller coaster. They experience a low and want to make a change, so they try to evoke better feelings through thinking positively. This generates a high. When done repeatedly and with conviction, the high can be tremendous. Remember, *thoughts produce emotions.* You can do this for days (as some workshops encourage) and feel ecstatic. But then, while you're waiting for the fruits of your mental labor to manifest, the underlying thought slowly reemerges. And as a result, you can feel even *more* depressed because not only are you not as successful as you had wanted to be, but you didn't manifest change properly and think you must be doing something wrong.

I'm not saying this happens to everyone. If you use positive thinking, the law of attraction, or another visualization technique and find that it consistently produces the change you seek in a way that is sustainable, great. I don't deny that it produces an immediate sense of empowerment, even exaltedness, because thoughts produce real feelings. And if you're using these amped-up thoughts and feelings to focus on short-term actions, you may be able to get things done effectively.

But when someone uses these tools as a long-term strategy for living happily, it can lead to a kind of bipolarism where the person continually soars and crashes, covering up their depression for fear of seeming like a failure. I've seen this repeatedly in people who later came to learn ActivInsight, and I know that therapists like Albert Ellis saw the same thing after *The Power of Positive Thinking* came out in the 1950s, when readers felt like they were doing everything they were instructed to do but still couldn't get reality to comply with their positive thoughts.

At its root, the problem comes down to how we deal with our negative thoughts about life. Positive thinking and the law of attraction encourage us to override or *not think* these thoughts, but that's like the old childhood game of not thinking about white bears, and suddenly all you can think about is white bears. Social psychologist Daniel M. Wegner, in his aptly titled book *White Bears and Other Unwanted Thoughts,* shares proof from his lab at Harvard that by trying *not* to think about something, you think about it *much more.* So the people trying to manifest more success or a better love life by *not* thinking in terms of failure or scarcity end up *sustaining* their negative beliefs, not eliminating them.

Positive thinking and the law of attraction aren't the only additive processes that can be problematic. Other examples are letting go, not taking things personally, and acceptance. There's nothing in your mind that lets something go if you still believe it. If you think that somebody hurt you, for example, saying that you'll "let the feelings go" is an exercise in either suppression or distraction. The feelings didn't arise as a result of choice or willpower, and they can't be released that way. They're there because they reflect your beliefs. Until those beliefs change, the emotions are bound to return.

Trying not to take something personally works (or doesn't work) the same way. Someone could say to you, "I think you're a worthless human being, but that's just my opinion. Don't take it personally." Good luck with that. People who tell themselves not to take something personally have already taken it personally, otherwise they wouldn't be making the attempt. Telling yourself not to believe something is futile if you already believe it.

And then there's acceptance, as in "That's just who my husband/wife/boss/coworker is, and I have to accept it." What we're really saying in these situations is that we wish we could change them, but we haven't figured out how. That's not acceptance. That's tolerance. Real acceptance is an open-armed, open-eyed embracing of the situation. To use the men from Phoenix House in chapter 2 as an example, many of them felt as if they had accepted their sentence before they did ActivInsight. But mentally they were still fighting it, so really they were just tolerating it. Only after working through their beliefs did they experience real acceptance. Acceptance is not resignation to your fate. It's a state of deep understanding and ease.

All these approaches—positive thinking, the law of attraction, letting go, not taking things personally, acceptance—are additive. They add a new layer of beliefs, emotions, or behaviors on top of whatever feels painful or limiting. This is intelligent because it does make a difference, but it goes only so far.

In contrast to the additive approaches, ActivInsight is what I call *subtractive*. Instead of adding positive beliefs to your mind, this process subtracts the negative ones already in place. When Dudley and his fellow residents believed, "I shouldn't be here," I didn't give them positive affirmations to repeat, tell them to make the best of the situation, or help them visualize how great things would be when they got out. That might have made them feel a little better, but the feeling wouldn't have lasted beyond the next time they had to clean the bathrooms.

Instead, we confronted their negative beliefs head on. And when they saw that those beliefs were untrue—that in reality they *should* be there at this time (because they did drugs and got arrested, etc.)—then their experience shifted at a much deeper level. They didn't have to *add* a positive belief. They *subtracted* a negative one, and felt far lighter for it. The same is true for subtracting beliefs such as, "There shouldn't be so much traffic," or "They shouldn't get so angry." Through insight, the weight of stressful thoughts falls away.

This is the nature of peace. Peace isn't something you get to by adding shiny new beliefs to your mind. Peace is what is left behind when the limiting, old beliefs have fallen away. I like to compare this subtractive approach to sunlight and clouds. With Activ-Insight, when things feel dark, you don't add sunlight (such as pep talks and motivation). Instead, you remove the clouds and find that the sun was already there. Or, for a more mechanical description, if your life doesn't feel as if it's moving forward, you don't try to step on the gas harder. Instead, you notice that the brakes were engaged without your realizing it, and you release them. That's how a subtractive process works. You remove what was blocking you so you can go faster with less effort. Now, if you wanted to add positive thinking or motivation *after* having an insight so that you become even more enthusiastic, so much the better. That way, there's no self-deception or denial underneath it. You're applying fresh paint to solid wood.

This process of subtraction is not a function of choice. You can't *choose* to think differently. What you can do, however, is examine your thoughts more closely. When you investigate a stressful belief and see that what you had thought to be true is, in fact, false, that belief falls away. In this sense, you don't hold stressful beliefs. They hold you. And they release their hold when you see that they're not true. Real psychological transformation doesn't happen through willpower, motivation, sincerity, or desire. It happens as you learn to distinguish between what's true and what's false, using the real world as proof. The more you do this, the more stressful beliefs you subtract from your mind, and your life.

As powerful as a subtractive approach can be, there are times when additive processes are completely appropriate and when a subtractive process may not be. When my father died, I didn't want someone to help me challenge my beliefs about life and death. I wanted a shoulder to cry on. And today if my friends complain about something going on in their lives, I'm far more likely to just listen and say a few encouraging words than to give them an ActivInsight worksheet. But when someone explicitly asks to go deeper, or when a client brings me in to teach the dynamics of real resilience, my approach is strictly subtractive, because in my experience that has the deepest effect and the greatest lasting value. You'll see this in the next chapter, where we explore the nature of uncertainty.

CHAPTER 11

The Myth
of Uncertainty

Mergers. Layoffs. Health challenges. Job security. Your financial future. Your romantic future. The future of life on Earth. According to media reports, we are living in the age of uncertainty, and people are experiencing unprecedented stress as a result.

This is complete nonsense.

If human beings actually experienced stress as a result of uncertainty, we would all be dead, because we live surrounded by more uncertainty than any of us can possibly fathom. Outside your window, billions of people are acting in ways that you can't control. Forces of nature are moving in ways that you can't anticipate. And trillions of cells within your body are interacting in ways that you don't even acknowledge, much less comprehend. We are tiny specks of presumption suspended in a vast universe of uncertainty.

And yet all this uncertainty has absolutely no power to make you feel anxious, insecure, or stressed out. Your thoughts about uncertainty trouble you, not uncertainty itself. And *this* means that there's hope, because your thoughts are something you can work with much more easily than the universe itself.

The worksheet that we're about to do together is shorter than the ones we've done so far, but don't let the short length fool you.

We are now in the intermediate section of part 2, the blue trails on the ski mountain. This requires a depth of honesty that most people will have to stretch a bit to reach. You'll see what I mean as we go through it. You're going to have to see for yourself whether or not uncertainty really is stressful, even if the whole world says that it is.

To give you an example of what this involves, let me share Tom's story. The bank that Tom worked for was in the throes of a messy acquisition. At times it wasn't clear if the merger was going to go through, or what the ramifications would be. Tens of thousands of employees, and the newspapers reporting on this from around the world, said that the uncertainty was unbearable. As you'll see shortly, Tom's experience suggests otherwise.

The statement we're going to work on is "I need to know what's going to happen to me." Write it on your worksheet now.

1 Write a concise, complete sentence describing something that you experience as stressful. It's helpful to use the words "should" or "shouldn't." (Ex.: "They should listen to me.")

> *I need to know what's going to happen to me.*

Then find a specific aspect of your life in which you feel bothered by uncertainty. It could be about your health, your career, your relationship, or your life's purpose. Whatever you think you need to know about, focus on that part, and write your worksheet mentally from there. Then ask yourself how strongly you feel this thought to be true. If you can find something above a 7, great. If not, is there something else in your past you were more anxious about? Take a moment to look, then circle your response in Step 2.

2 How strongly do you feel this belief to be true?

0 1 2 3 4 5 6 7 8 9 10

⟶ stronger

Next, when you think this thought, "I need to know what's going to happen to me," how do you feel? Tom circled *anxious, helpless, impatient,* and *tense.* Circle or write in the emotions that come up for you.

3a How do you **feel** when you believe this?
(Circle below or add your own.)

afraid   abandoned   angry   annoyed   anxious

confused   depressed   desperate   embarrassed

frustrated   helpless   hopeless   hurt   impatient

inadequate   insecure   invisible   jealous   nervous

rejected   resentful   tense   upset   worried

When you feel this way, how do you act in that moment? Is that when you procrastinate? Do you eat differently? Do you treat others differently? Do you imagine worst-case scenarios over and over, living out your own personal doomsday? Be thorough. This is your life. Take a good look at it. Tom found himself complaining, losing focus, procrastinating, and worrying constantly. What actions describe your behavior?

3b How do you **act** when you feel this way?
(Circle below or add your own.)

argue   belittle   blame   bully   complain   cry   drink

eat   escape   fight   find fault with   give up   gossip

insult   interrupt   lose sleep   manipulate   obsess

overwork   pity myself   preach   pretend   procrastinate

shop   shut down   smoke   suffer   withdraw   yell

Next, write the negation. What's the negation for "I need to know what's going to happen to me"? The answer is:

---

4 Write the negation of your statement from Step 1. In most cases, you also add "In reality" at the beginning and "at this time" or "at that time" at the end.

> *In reality, at this time I don't need to know what's going to*

happen to me.

I moved *at this time* toward the front because if it came at the end of the sentence, you could think it referred to what was happening at this time instead of what you need at this time.

So can you think of any way in which it's true that in reality at this time, you *don't* need to know what's going to happen to you? If you were a lawyer whose sole job was to find proof for that statement, what could you come up with? Pause to think about it for a few minutes, writing down what you find, then continue to the paragraph below.

There are just three suggested proofs for this negation, given below with Tom's feedback:

In reality, at this time I don't need to know what's going to happen to me because I can survive this moment without knowing.

Give this one a chance to sink in. This is what "need" means. You physically need something in order to live. You need air. You need water. You need food. You don't "need" to know what's going to happen to you. You *want* to know, but that's a very different thought.

Psychologist Albert Ellis repeatedly pointed out the difference between "want" and "need" decades ago, and Byron Katie has done the same more recently, but most of us still confuse the two and experience stress as a result. This makes it much harder to focus on what we have to do right now. "I really thought I *needed* to know," Tom said. "But the truth is, I can get through this moment without knowing. I've gotten through several weeks of not knowing, and I'm still here. So I don't need to know. I want to know."

Reflect on your own experience and see if you find this proof to be true. If so, add it to your worksheet, then continue to the next suggestions.

In reality, at this time I don't need to know what's going to happen to me because I still have things to do for now. (Specify what.)

We often think we need to know what's going to happen to us in order to take the next step, but in reality the next step is clear.

When you're not telling yourself and everyone else that you need to know what's going to happen, you can focus on the step in front of you, whether it's completing an ongoing project, brushing up your CV, following doctors' orders, filling out applications, or simply getting some rest while you wait things out. But can you see that, just for this moment, you have things to do, and that this is part of why you don't *need* to know more?

"I don't *need* to know," Tom said, "because what I have to do, I have to do anyway. My day-to-day responsibilities are still in effect. I have the same calls to make, the same numbers to run. My group could keep doing what we do for months. So this is true for me. At this time, part of why I don't need to know what's going to happen to me is that, right now, I have plenty to do."

If this is true for you, add it to your worksheet, then consider the final suggestion.

In reality, at this time I don't need to know what's going to happen to me because in this moment, I'm actually okay.

Take a little time with this one. You may have fears about what you believe is going to happen, but can you see that right now, in this moment, you're doing okay? This doesn't mean that you're feeling great, nor does it mean that you want this sense of uncertainty to last. But if you're going to be completely honest with yourself, you're still alive, you have things to do, and you're okay. That's proof that you don't absolutely need to know what will happen, and it goes on your list.

"This one is also true for me," Tom noted. "In my group, we've all been acting like we're mortally wounded, but the truth is, I still have my job. I'm getting paid. I have some money saved up. For this moment, I don't need to know what's going to happen to me. Right now, I'm okay."

Here's our proof listed together. Read it out loud to yourself:

5 Write below all the proof you can find that supports the negation being true in reality at this time (or in the past). Don't rush. Be thorough, using an additional sheet of paper if necessary.

> In reality, at this time I don't need to know what's going to happen to me because I can survive this moment without knowing.

> In reality, at this time I don't need to know what's going to happen to me because I still have things to do for now. (Specify what.)

> In reality, at this time I don't need to know what's going to happen to me because in this moment, I'm actually okay.

When you realize that you may *want* to know what will happen but that you don't *need* to know, how do you feel? "Much more composed," Tom said. "I feel more patient, and more relaxed. I do still want to know what will happen, but right now I have a job, I have a supportive family, I have some cash set aside, and I feel okay. I can do this."

Describe what you feel using the list in Step 6a.

6a How do you *feel* when you see the truth of the negation? (Circle below or add your own.)

calm   clear   compassionate   connected   curious

enlightened   enthusiastic   excited   free   grateful

honest   humble   intimate   light   loving   optimistic

peaceful   playful   relaxed   relieved   serene

supportive   tolerant   truthful   understanding

And when you feel this way, what might you do? What actions can you take?

"I can stay focused," Tom said. "I can do my job and help people in my group do theirs. I'll still check in to see what our fate may hold, but in the meantime, we have work to do. I'm going to make sure we do it."

What actions seem appropriate to you? Fill them in on your worksheet in Step 6b.

6b What **actions** might come from this?
(Circle below or add your own.)

accept   apologize   approach   be honest   breathe

clarify   communicate   contribute   delegate   exercise

explore   focus   follow through   forgive   give thanks

listen   make amends   network   open up   participate

prioritize   reach out   share   speak up   support

Make sure you put these actions into motion. People who believe that they need to know what's going to happen to them are frequently paralyzed. People who realize that they don't need to know what's going to happen release that frozen energy. Use it.

Finally, how true does the original statement, "I need to know what's going to happen to me," seem now? You may *want* to know, but do you really *need* to know?

7 Read your original statement again. How strongly do you feel this belief to be true now?

0 1 2 3 4 5 6 7 8 9 10

weaker ⟵ —————————

Did you go down in points? If so, well done. "Need" statements can be tricky because of the way we typically misuse language, but when you resolve a "need" into a "want," it always results in a lighter feeling, because believing that you need something you don't is inherently stressful.

If you still feel frustrated, it's most likely because you have other related beliefs that are still contracted. Stressful beliefs tend to form clusters, so that you have a small grouping of thoughts on the same issue. Examples of a cluster related to this topic are thoughts such as: "I should know what's going to happen by now," "I shouldn't have to wait to find out what will happen," and "This shouldn't be happening." Any or all of these are worth working on. What you'll find as you transform this cluster through insight is that your mind becomes increasingly clear and you feel more comfortable with not knowing for the time being.

Is this a form of denial? Actually, it's the exact opposite of denial. It's seeing the truth: you don't know what will happen. Most people deny this truth by pretending that they *do* know what will happen and that *it will be bad*. Listen to how frequently people say, "I don't know" as if it's a negative statement. "Oh," they say with a deep sigh, "I just don't know what will happen." But not knowing isn't negative. It's simply an absence. Only when you subconsciously think, "I need to know" or "I should know by now" do you feel a contraction, and you then contaminate the space of not knowing with your negative assumptions.

You'll notice this frequently in politics, where those who are against a change will emphasize how this "might" or "could" lead to some disaster, and the outcome is "unknown." See reality clearly and you won't fall prey to these tactics. The unknown is not a scary place. That would disqualify it from being unknown. Uncertainty and the unknown are completely nonthreatening unless you imagine that you know something you don't. Then the fear begins.

In the context of this particular worksheet topic, understanding the difference between what you need and what you don't need enables you to dispel this fear and take action or wait with equal poise. It also turns you into an example of clarity for those still struggling with their own uncertainty (which is really their *certainty* that something negative is going to happen). This is what happened to Tom, who began this worksheet feeling stressed-out and preoccupied. He started at an 8 and ended at a 0, noticing a marked change in how he thought about his situation.

This, in turn, immediately changed how he felt. Tom experienced no emotional impact during the transition, while his colleagues who didn't do ActivInsight suffered enormously. Tom remained peaceful at home as well, with none of the tension and fighting that his coworkers reported. He was able to stay focused and get his work done.

When the acquiring bank finally announced its new structure, Tom was happy to learn that he was promoted to head of strategy for the entire brokerage organization. He sent me an email summing up his experience:

Doing ActivInsight worksheets fundamentally changed how I understood and handled stress. I went from an emotional to a rational approach, and instead of ignoring my stress or covering it up, I <u>eliminated</u> it. As a result, I could focus on what was in front of me in a healthy and productive way, which had a positive impact on my career, and continues to. I now keep a stack of worksheets in my top right desk drawer and pull them out as needed, and I am a strong advocate of this process.

This may seem like a large shift for such a small distinction, but relatively small differences in how you think can result in profound changes in how you feel and how you act.

As more companies merge in order to stay competitive and the global economy keeps changing, you will most likely continue to hear that uncertainty is stressful, and millions of people will panic based on what's taking place not in their surroundings but in their heads. Thankfully, through insight, you have the ability to remain steady, and that can give you leverage to help the rest of us.

CHAPTER 12

The Myth of a Broken Heart

After a very messy breakup with her ex, Ricardo, Sabrina couldn't stop crying. In her words, she "felt like somebody threw a fishing hook down my throat, ripped out my heart, and left a shell." When Sabrina then ran into Ricardo with his tall, blond new girlfriend at a club, she went into a tailspin. Sabrina had struggled with addiction in the past, and somewhere between the crying and the drugs, she realized that she needed to find a more constructive way to deal with her heartbreak. That way turned out to be ActivInsight.

It would sound impressive to say that Sabrina did one worksheet on her breakup and that was it—the tears dried up, she was over Ricardo and moved on. But that's not usually how it works. There are no magic bullets. A big issue like heartbreak might involve a dozen or more different thoughts, such as "I'm worthless. I'm not attractive enough. Nobody will ever love me again. I did something wrong"—and really clearing this up means looking at all of them. Each completed worksheet builds on the others, or, to put it more accurately, each *un*builds, so that little by little the mental contractions that produce the pain disappear.

Sabrina and I sat down with a box of Kleenex, a stack of worksheets, and her dog. I listened for half an hour as Sabrina told me the story of Ricardo, and I jotted down the stressful beliefs I could hear in her thought process. Once these were all on paper, I read them out loud to her and asked her to identify the ones that were the most charged. That's where we began. We did this every day for four days. Sabrina went through a lot of tissues, and a lot of worksheets. This was not easy, but at the end of it, she found herself in a startlingly different place.

To get the most value out of this chapter, think of someone in your life who broke your heart. It could have happened recently, or it could have happened many years ago, but somewhere in your mind put a name and a face on this belief. Then write on the lines of Step 1, "I want him back" or "I want her back." Even if it's no longer true, do it mentally and emotionally from the time when it was. By personalizing this worksheet to your own experience, this chapter becomes not just a story, but a journey.

Fill out Step 1 now.

---

1 Write a concise, complete sentence describing something that you experience as stressful. It's helpful to use the words "should" or "shouldn't." (Ex.: "They should listen to me.")

> *I want him back.*

In Step 2, rate how strongly you believe this to be true. Remember to put yourself in the place where you most strongly feel it. If you're working on an old flame and have trouble getting the feeling back strongly, I have a suggestion. Listen to the song "Crying," by Roy Orbison, as sung by k.d. lang. Then, when the feelings for "I want him back" are more present, circle the number on your worksheet that feels right.

For Sabrina, this belief couldn't have been stronger. "I want him back physically," she said. "I don't just mean sex, though, damn, I want that back, too. But I want to just feel him next to me. That's what I miss the most. His presence."

She rated it a 10. Circle the number that feels right to you.

---

2 How strongly do you feel this belief to be true?

0 1 2 3 4 5 6 7 8 9 10

⟶ stronger

Next, how do you feel when you think this thought, "I want him back"?

"I feel almost every feeling on here," Sabrina said, circling a dozen different emotions. "I feel like a rejected sack of shit. You don't have that on here, so I'm writing it in."

Add any necessary feelings to your worksheet.

3a How do you *feel* when you believe this?
(Circle below or add your own.)

afraid   abandoned   angry   annoyed   anxious

confused   depressed   desperate   embarrassed

frustrated   helpless   hopeless   hurt   impatient

inadequate   insecure   invisible   jealous   nervous

rejected   resentful   tense   upset   worried

In Step 3b, when you feel the way you just wrote down, how do you act?

"I cry, obviously," Sabrina said, taking another tissue. "I tell myself I'm worthless. I pity myself. I get high. I call him and beg him to come back. It's not pretty."

It doesn't have to be pretty. What do *you* do? If you're working on something from the past, push yourself to remember what you did. Did you try to persuade or manipulate him? Did you lie or pretend to be different so that she would come back? Be as honest and thorough as you can be.

3b How do you **act** when you feel this way?
(Circle below or add your own.)

argue   belittle   blame   bully   complain   cry   drink

eat   escape   fight   find fault with   give up   gossip

insult   interrupt   lose sleep   manipulate   obsess

overwork   pity myself   preach   pretend   procrastinate

shop   shut down   smoke   suffer   withdraw   yell

In Step 4, what's the negation for "I want him back"?

Sabrina said, "'In reality, I don't want him back at this time.' But that's not true."

It may seem not the least bit true, but write it down.

4 Write the negation of your statement from Step 1. In most cases, you also add "In reality" at the beginning and "at this time" or "at that time" at the end.

> *In reality, I don't want him back at this time.*

_____

_____

In Step 5, your job is to try to find any and all legitimate proof for why the negation is true. Can you think of any ways in which you don't want him (or her) back at this time? Pause to think about it for yourself, then read through my exchange with Sabrina.

"Can you think of any ways in which it's true in reality that you don't want him back at this time?" I asked Sabrina.

"Yeah," she said sarcastically. "In reality, I don't want him back at this time because he's a pig."

Anytime you come up with a strong judgment of yourself or others while doing this step, you want to drill down to the underlying evidence that judgment is built on. I pointed this out to Sabrina and asked her why Ricardo was a pig.

"Because he's already screwing that blond bimbo from the club," she said.

"Got it. So in reality you don't want him back at this time because he's sleeping with another woman?"

"Right," Sabrina said. "I'm so pissed off at him for that. I mean, I don't know that they're sleeping together—I don't want to think about it—but how could he bring her there? He knows I go to that club. He's such a bastard. He really is a bastard. I'm not drilling down on that one."

189

"Okay, let's write that first one on your worksheet and keep going."

Sabrina wrote on her worksheet:

- *In reality, I don't want him back at this time because he's already dating another woman.*

"What else?" I asked.

Sabrina thought for a moment.

"In reality, I don't want him back at this time because he's an asshole for dumping me. Except that's not true, I do want him back. But he is an asshole for dumping me."

"How could you go a little bit deeper into that one?" I asked.

"Do you mean that you want me to pretend that I don't want him back when I do?"

"No," I explained. "I don't want you to pretend. But it may be that part of you wants him back, and part of you doesn't. I want to hear from that other part. How could that part rephrase the proof you just came up with?"

"Oh, I see," she said. "I do feel like that, like part of me wants him back and part of me doesn't. So . . . in reality, I don't want him back at this time because . . . I think the 'asshole' refers to the fact that I don't really trust him after what happened. I don't think I would feel as good around him."

"Good. Write both of those down."

Sabrina added to her worksheet:

- *In reality, I don't want him back at this time because I don't really trust him after what happened.*
- *In reality, I don't want him back at this time because I don't think I would feel as good around him.*

"What else?" I asked.

There was a long pause. "I don't know," Sabrina said, starting to cry again. "The thing is, I do want him back . . . I think. I'm confused. I can't think of any other reasons why I would not want him back. I wish I didn't want him back, but I do. I need help."

"Well, I'll make a suggestion," I said, "and you tell me if it gives you any more ideas. Let's imagine that we could transport Ricardo here now. So here he is. But he's not the Ricardo of your fantasies, here to apologize and shower you with love and affection. He's the Ricardo of reality, the one who broke up with you but is just suddenly placed here. What do you think would happen?"

"I know exactly what would happen," Sabrina said, "because it happened last week when I asked him to come over to talk. He would tell me that he's really sorry that I'm so upset, that he didn't mean to hurt me, and then I would get irrational and he would make some excuse to leave."

"Okay, so, is *that* someone you want to date?"

"No. I want someone who wants to be with me." It took a second for Sabrina to realize what she had said. "Oh, that's another proof! In reality, I don't want him back at this time because I want to be with someone who really wants to be with me. That's true!"

"Very good. So write that down."

- *In reality, I don't want him back at this time because I want to be with someone who really wants to be with me.*

After writing it, Sabrina looked up. "I don't understand," she said. "This is totally true, but I still feel like I want him back so badly. Why? Am I crazy?"

"Keep going and let's see what happens," I said. "Can you think of any other reasons why it would be true that you don't want him back at this time?"

Sabrina was quiet for a minute.

"I'm thinking," she said, "about something you just said, about Ricardo suddenly being here, but as he really is, not as my fantasy version. When I think of him as Real Ricardo and not Fantasy Ricardo, when I think of him as someone who doesn't truly want to be with me, I *don't* really want him back. I mean, I'm not trying to trap him here. But then I think that he should still want to be with me."

"Aha," I said. "Okay. Hang on to this worksheet. We're going to come right back to it, but let's get another worksheet out first."

There will be times when you're doing ActivInsight that you feel the statement you're working on start to loosen, and a different thought seems to take its place more strongly. When that happens, you can do one of two things. You can either finish the worksheet you started and then do the second one, or you can temporarily suspend the first one and jump to the second one, and then come back. I opted for us to do the latter, because sometimes it can have a dynamic cumulative effect. You can finish your present worksheet, or follow along with Sabrina.

Sabrina got out a second worksheet and moved quickly through it. "Ricardo should still want to be with me," she wrote. "That's a 10. I feel angry, frustrated, hurt, inadequate, insecure, and rejected. I cry, I pout, I try to make him want to be with me, I tempt him sexually, I throw tantrums, I get high, I try to get a mutual friend to convince him to come back to me, I shut down, I beat myself up, I see myself as worthless, I see life as worthless."

"Good work. What's the negation?" I asked.

"In reality, Ricardo should not still want to be with me at this time."

"Right. Okay, now I want you to look at Ricardo, but not

through your eyes. Look at him from high overhead, as if you're a cloud floating above the world. You see his life, his needs, his interests, his habits. And you see yourself, your life, your needs. From that vantage point, why is it true that in reality, Ricardo should not still want to be with you at this time?"

Sabrina took a deep breath. "You do realize that this is killing me," she said.

"Part of you. I do. Insight is always a death, the dying of what we believed. But that's what makes room for the truth. So what do you see?"

She took another deep breath.

"In reality, Ricardo should not still want to be with me at this time . . . because . . . because he and I want different things."

Sabrina started crying again, but it was a different kind of crying. It seemed like she had realized something important.

"We want different things," she said. "I know it. We even talked about it a little at the beginning, but I wanted to pretend that it wasn't true."

"So how would you write that?" I asked. It may seem harsh that I would push someone crying to keep writing, but the writing is important. It helps the mind fully focus.

"In reality," Sabrina wrote, "Ricardo should not still want to be with me at this time because we want different things, and he knows that."

"Can you be more specific?" I asked.

She said, "Well, he wants to enjoy being together, having sex, going dancing, and having fun. And I want that, too, believe me. But I also want a real relationship. I'm ready for that. I want a family, or at least to keep my options open."

"Add that to your worksheet in parentheses so you know exactly what 'different things' means when you review it."

Sabrina wrote it down. Usually when you're doing a worksheet, you want to spend time looking for all the proof you can in Step 5, but in this case it seemed to me that we could move on. Sabrina could always go back to Step 5 later and add more proof, but it felt like she got the main insight she needed. If you're doing the second worksheet, you can look for more proof before rejoining us.

"In Step 6, how do you feel when you see that?" I asked.

"Sad. Why isn't that on here?"

"Because we have to be a little more focused. The thought that we're working on is, 'In reality, Ricardo should not still want to be with me at this time.' Sadness might come from thinking that you're not going to be together, or that he's not the one, or that it should have worked out. But when you focus just on the negation and what you realized, what feeling do you have?"

"Oh," she said. "I see. Yeah, when I focus just on the realization that in reality, he shouldn't still want to be with me now, I feel . . . honest. That feels much more honest. And I feel kind of relieved."

"Why?"

"Because it's like I don't have to play this game anymore. I don't have to pretend that I don't want something serious and act more casual than I want to be."

"That makes sense to me. What else do you feel?"

"Calm. I feel calm. I'm not crying anymore."

"That's true," I said. "What else?"

"I feel connected. I feel more connected to who he really is, whereas before I think I was trying to connect to my fantasy version, which was impossible because it wasn't even real."

"That's a good insight. How about actions? What might you do, feeling relieved, calm, and connected to him?"

She looked over Step 6b. "Accept. Accept his decision. Apologize for some of the shit I put him through. Be honest about our different needs. Breathe. Communicate. Forgive. I do forgive him.

I mean, Christ, what did he do? He told me how he felt. And really, I knew that we were different that way from the start. I thought maybe I could be how I used to be, or that he would grow into wanting something else."

"I'm sure that would sound familiar to a lot of people, including me. Let's go to the last step. Ricardo should still want to be with you. In reality, how true is that on a scale from 0 to 10?"

Sabrina thought about it for a while.

"I'm going to give it a 3," she said.

"That's a big move, 10 to 3. I would review that whole worksheet later, but let's jump back to the first one now. Look over what you wrote in Step 5 on your first worksheet."

"I want to change something," Sabrina said, reading what she had written on her first worksheet. "It's not that I don't trust him. It's more like I don't want him back because . . . he doesn't belong to me now. Maybe he never really did, but I thought he did, or was willing to pretend. But now I can't."

"Good find. Okay, change that. Is there another proof you can add?"

"Yeah." She started writing, "In reality, I don't want him back at this time because we're in different places, and I want someone who shares my desire for a serious relationship."

"Yes," I said. "That's the missing piece from the other worksheet."

"Damn," she said. "This is good shit!"

"You're doing really well," I said. "Read it out loud."

---

5 Write below all the proof you can find that supports the negation being true in reality at this time (or in the past). Don't rush. Be thorough, using an additional sheet of paper if necessary.

> In reality, I don't want him back at this time because he's already dating another woman.

> In reality, I don't want him back at this time because I know that he doesn't really belong to me now.

> In reality, I don't want him back at this time because I don't think I would feel as good around him.

> In reality, I don't want him back at this time because I want to be with someone who really wants to be with me.

> In reality, I don't want him back at this time because we're in different places, and I want someone who shares my desire for a serious relationship.

"How about Step 6?" I asked. "How do you feel looking over Step 5 and seeing the negation as true?"

6a How do you **feel** when you see the truth of the negation? (Circle below or add your own.)

calm   clear   compassionate   connected   curious
enlightened   enthusiastic   excited   free   grateful
honest   humble   intimate   light   loving   optimistic
peaceful   playful   relaxed   relieved   serene
supportive   tolerant   truthful   understanding

"I feel calmer, clearer, more compassionate . . . I feel almost everything on here. Maybe not serene, but most of these other words. I feel totally different than I did before."

196

"And action steps?" Look over your own worksheet.

6b What *actions* might come from this?
(Circle below or add your own.)

accept   apologize   approach   be honest   breathe

clarify   communicate   contribute   delegate   exercise

explore   focus   follow through   forgive   give thanks

listen   make amends   network   open up   participate

prioritize   reach out   share   speak up   support

"I want to be honest with Ricardo," Sabrina said, "and with myself. I want to open up. And I want to find someone who wants the same thing I want . . . and is great in bed, of course."

"Of course," I said. "So: 'I want him back.' Real Ricardo, not Fantasy Ricardo. Ricardo as he actually is, the Ricardo who ended the relationship you were in. How true is it that you want him back?" Ask yourself this as you fill out Step 7.

7 Read your original statement again. How strongly do you feel this belief to be true now?

0   1   2   3   4   5   6   7   8   9   10

weaker ⟵━━━━━━━

"It's not true at all," she said, "but I'm circling 1 because I feel like I still have some beliefs about this kicking around in me. But I really don't want that Ricardo back. Jesus, I can't believe I did this."

Sabrina cleaned up the tissues and we chatted about her insights for a while. She was tired, as she ought to have been. When you do ActivInsight for real, it's a workout. It can be just as exhausting as a physical workout, and just as rewarding. I suggested that she go for a walk with her dog to get some air and move around, and review her worksheets later in the day. If you experienced insights on your own worksheet as you followed along, I would suggest the same to you.

Sabrina and I did other worksheets together as different thoughts came up. Each time, she put everything she could into each step, especially Step 5. Then, shortly after our series of private sessions ended, she ran into Ricardo with yet another woman and was amazed that not only did she not die a thousand deaths, but they all had a good time together. A week later, she emailed me to say that Ricardo had slept over at her house. "There was no monkey business!" Sabrina wrote. "We just talked, and it was a beautiful experience of trust and closeness. I feel like I'm seeing people and things as they really are for the first time, and as a result, my life is opening up in incredible ways."

At the same time, Sabrina got clearer on what she really wanted from a relationship. And, to her great surprise, she found herself uninterested in men who would have interested her previously, and attracted to a man who was different from anyone she had dated before. Today, they're happily married with a beautiful daughter, and Sabrina still does ActivInsight when anything bothers her.

Millions of people around the world struggle as Sabrina did with what we call heartbreak, but the truth is that no one is ever heartbroken. What we really are is *thoughtbroken.* Our most deeply held beliefs are what cause our pain: "He should still want to be with me." "She shouldn't have left me." "I want him back." Throughout all of it, our hearts pump away, unscathed. But our thoughts are a broken and bleeding mess.

The remedy is to unbreak not your heart, but your head. Find the stressful thoughts that you have about your relationship, write them down, and start challenging them. Use Sabrina's moxie and intelligence as inspiration. Anyone can do this and, with some effort and diligence, see a real change. I know this because of what followed.

A few months after working with Sabrina, I got a call from Anne, a friend of hers, who had seen how well Sabrina was doing and wanted to explore a relationship challenge of her own. Actually, Anne had several challenges. She had been diagnosed as paranoid schizophrenic years before. As a result, she was on heavy medication, and her doctors told her that she would never be able to think clearly and would always be mentally unstable. Her marriage was falling apart, and she was warned against having children because of her obsessive thoughts. To be honest, I wasn't sure she would be able to do ActivInsight on the issues she described. But Sabrina was sure it could help, Anne's therapist was very supportive, and Anne herself wanted to try. What happened surprised me.

Not only could Anne do ActivInsight, but she was one of the most skillful practitioners I've ever seen. After doing a few worksheets with me, she knew intuitively exactly how to phrase her statements, and was both creative and thorough when proving the negations. She went through these steps beautifully, like a dancer. It was a joy to watch her.

Anne went off to do worksheets on her own, and we lost touch. We reconnected years later during the writing of this book, when she sent me the following update:

> After learning to do ActivInsight with you, I did over one hundred worksheets over the course of the next year, in addition to exploring nutritional protocols that would help strengthen and balance me mentally. As a result, I was able to break down my

old mental models and negate the beliefs that I had. The old train tracks grew over and I can't believe I was ever considered crippled. I am healthy, happy, and sound. My eighteen-year marriage has finally blossomed into a true partnership, whereas before Activ-Insight it had a caregiver/invalid dynamic. We now have twin toddlers, and life is a joyful adventure with exciting challenges and a whole lot of sweet peace.

Anne's story may be extraordinary, but the dynamics of stress and peace work the same for all of us. Find your contracted thoughts, challenge them, and unbreak your head.

CHAPTER 13

The Myth of Having Too Much To Do

I have too much to do. How can this not be stressful? It's not possible to have this much to do and not experience stress. Besides, the stress helps me get stuff done. Right?"

Charles, a senior vice president at a Fortune 100 company, could be speaking for all of us. On the Top Ten list of stressful phrases, "I have too much to do" always ranks close to the top. It doesn't matter what you do, whether you're a captain of industry or a soccer mom or both—your plate is full with work, family, and whatever passes for a social life, and you're already using the largest plate you can find.

But how is it possible to have "too much" to do? Is the universe going to implode because the distribution of responsibilities has become imbalanced around you? Are you about to die as a result of your to-do list? In reality, no one has "too much" to do. They have what they have. It may be so much that it would take days, weeks, or months to get through it all, but it's still not "too much." It's just a lot.

But when you tell yourself, "I have too much to do," even though that belief is false, the stress it produces is very real.

That's how stress works. You believe something that has no factual basis in reality, but the effect is very much a fact, with measurable consequences. Your emotional struggle is real. The changes in your behavior are real. The hormones disturbing your bloodstream are real. Thoughts, even when they're not true, are powerful things.

Thankfully, so are insights. When you realize that you don't really have too much to do (you just have a lot to do), your mind and body relax a little, and that thought loses its ability to stick. "All right, fine," you say, begrudgingly. "I don't have 'too much' to do. I'm not going to die from this and the universe won't implode. But still, *I shouldn't have so much to do.*"

Now *that's* a belief worth exploring. Get out a worksheet, and let's take a closer look together.

On the lines of Step 1, write, "I shouldn't have so much to do."

1 Write a concise, complete sentence describing something that you experience as stressful. It's helpful to use the words "should" or "shouldn't." (Ex.: "They should listen to me.")

> *I shouldn't have so much to do.*

_____

_____

In Step 2, how strongly do you believe this to be true? Find the place in your mind from which you most strongly believe it, and then circle the number that feels right to you.

2 How strongly do you feel this belief to be true?

0   1   2   3   4   5   6   7   8   9   10

———————————————▶ stronger

In Step 3, when you think to yourself, "I shouldn't have so much to do," how do you feel? Tired? Resentful? Stretched too thin? Look over the list on your worksheet, and circle or write in the feelings that ring true to you.

3a How do you *feel* when you believe this?
(Circle below or add your own.)

afraid   abandoned   angry   annoyed   anxious

confused   depressed   desperate   embarrassed

frustrated   helpless   hopeless   hurt   impatient

inadequate   insecure   invisible   jealous   nervous

rejected   resentful   tense   upset   worried

Next, when you feel the way you just described, how do you act? Some people drink, some people smoke, some people contemplate quitting. A lot of people complain and lose sleep. What do you do?

3b How do you *act* when you feel this way?
(Circle below or add your own.)

argue   belittle   blame   bully   complain   cry   drink

eat   escape   fight   find fault with   give up   gossip

insult   interrupt   lose sleep   manipulate   obsess

overwork   pity myself   preach   pretend   procrastinate

shop   shut down   smoke   suffer   withdraw   yell

What's the negation for "I shouldn't have so much to do"? Write it on the lines of Step 4.

4 Write the negation of your statement from Step 1. In most cases, you also add "In reality" at the beginning and "at this time" or "at that time" at the end.

> *In reality, I should have so much to do at this time.*

_____

_____

Now let's prove it. How could the negation possibly be true? See what you can come up with on your own, then I'll make some suggestions for you to consider.

Here is some possible proof for why, in reality, you should have so much to do at this time. The list is long, but read it over slowly and see what insights it gives you for your own worksheet.

5 Write below all the proof you can find that supports the negation being true in reality at this time (or in the past). Don't rush. Be thorough, using an additional sheet of paper if necessary.

> *In reality, I should have so much to do at this time because that's what they pay me for.*

> *In reality, I should have so much to do at this time because I'm the low man on the totem pole at work and have to pick up other people's slack.*

> *In reality, I should have so much to do at this time because I'm in a senior position, and that comes with additional responsibilities.*

> *In reality, I should have so much to do at this time because I want to prove to myself or others that I can handle a lot. (Specify who.)*

> *In reality, I should have so much to do at this time because if I didn't have a lot to do, I wouldn't think as highly of myself.*

> *In reality, I should have so much to do at this time because staying really busy helps me avoid dealing with other problems in my life.*

> *In reality, I should have so much to do at this time because I believe that what I'm doing must be done now, no matter the personal cost.*

> *In reality, I should have so much to do at this time because I don't prioritize well. I think that everything is equally important.*

> In reality, I should have so much to do at this time because I'm not good at saying no when people ask me to do something.

> In reality, I should have so much to do at this time because I think that the more I take on, the more I'll be appreciated.

> In reality, I should have so much to do at this time because I am not very organized in how I use my time and energy.

> In reality, I should have so much to do at this time because I've been procrastinating.

> In reality, I should have so much to do at this time because I work in a culture that glorifies working long hours.

> In reality, I should have so much to do at this time because I want to excel at multiple things, each of which is very demanding.

> In reality, I should have so much to do at this time because I don't have anyone who can help me.

> In reality, I should have so much to do at this time because I haven't taken the time to train someone else properly to handle some of my responsibilities.

> In reality, I should have so much to do at this time because I think that if I ask for help, I will seem weak.

> In reality, I should have so much to do at this time because I tell myself it's not possible to hand off some of my responsibilities, and this limits me from coming up with creative solutions.

> In reality, I should have so much to do at this time because I believe that I do things better than other people would, so I take everything on myself.

> _In reality, I should have so much to do at this time because_
> _I believe that who I am is defined by what I do._

As this worksheet makes clear, what separates doing ActivInsight from _really_ doing ActivInsight is how hard you throw yourself into Step 5, which invites you to push past your excuses and, in the words of Dudley from Phoenix House, get really real. When I'm coaching someone privately, I like to see that person fill out every line on the worksheet with proof, then fill a separate sheet of paper, and then fill the other side of that sheet of paper. _That's_ proving the negation. Sometimes people will actually feel woozy from the effort, as if their heads are spinning, but they see the negation as undeniably true because they've thoroughly proven it to themselves. Even years later, the negation will still ring true. The negation isn't something you make yourself believe. It's the truth you were missing, and doing this step helps you see it as clearly as the back of your hand.

This exhaustive thoroughness isn't possible for every negation— sometimes only a few pieces of proof make sense—but for a worksheet like this one, there are many reasons why you should have a lot to do at this time. And the more of these you identify, the deeper the shift that takes place.

Even when it's dramatic, though, this shift isn't always obvious to others. That's what I learned from Charles, mentioned at the start of this chapter. I had been invited to work with a group of very senior executives struggling with burnout (among other things) and was coaching the participants through several different worksheets related to their specific business challenges, including this one on "I shouldn't have so much to do." When they got to the negation, I asked if anyone could come up with why, in reality, they should have so much to do at this time.

There was dead silence.

I offered a few suggestions—their budgets had been cut, their head count was reduced, they couldn't outsource as freely—and they all started writing. No one said a word, but they kept writing for several minutes. I asked again if anyone wanted to share what they came up with.

More silence.

We went through the rest of the worksheet and completed the session. From looking at the faces of the thirty or so people in the room, I thought maybe they didn't get it at all. This process isn't for everyone. No process is. But I had never seen a roomful of people seem so unresponsive.

A few days later, the feedback forms came in—all incredibly positive, with most participants raving about the insights they had had. Charles, one of the participants, told me what had happened.

"You have to understand," he said, "we're in a group setting, we're all pretty senior, and the CEO is there. We're not going to say out loud that we're control freaks or that one of our direct reports screwed up and that's why we should have so much work at this time. But what's great about this tool is that we can all write down our insights privately and really own them without having to expose ourselves. And that's what we did."

I asked Charles how he felt after realizing that he *should* have so much work at this time.

"Fine," he said, laughing. "It's funny because I still have the exact same amount of work, but it's like a switch was flipped. Mentally I'm in a different place. My coworkers and my wife thank you."

When you can see clearly that you should have so much to do at this time for the reasons you've listed, what feelings come with that for you? Read your proof from Step 5 out loud if you haven't, and take it in slowly. Do you feel a sense of understanding? Acceptance? Honesty? Identify what emotions arise for you.

6a How do you *feel* when you see the truth of the negation? (Circle below or add your own.)

calm   clear   compassionate   connected   curious

enlightened   enthusiastic   excited   free   grateful

honest   humble   intimate   light   loving   optimistic

peaceful   playful   relaxed   relieved   serene

supportive   tolerant   truthful   understanding

When you feel this way, how might you act? What could you do, or what would you stop doing? See what you can come up with below.

6b What *actions* might come from this?
(Circle below or add your own.)

accept   apologize   approach   be honest   breathe

clarify   communicate   contribute   delegate   exercise

explore   focus   follow through   forgive   give thanks

listen   make amends   network   open up   participate

prioritize   reach out   share   speak up   support

And, finally, rate the original belief again. On a scale from 0 to 10, how true is it, in reality, that you should not have so much to do?

7 Read your original statement again. How strongly do you feel this belief to be true now?

0   1   2   3   4   5   6   7   8   9   10

weaker ←————————————

Good job completing another worksheet.

Before you go on to the next chapter, I want to expand on something Charles said. He said he still had the same amount of work, but he felt different. One argument that people sometimes make against ActivInsight is that we don't need to work on our thoughts—we need to work directly on the problems facing us in the world. Here's why I disagree.

When you experience a problem, such as believing you have too much to do, it triggers a cascade of hormones internally that, in turn, cause a larger chain reaction. You become angry or resentful, lash out at others or wallow in self-pity, and blame the world for your condition—all the effects you see in Step 3 on your worksheet. When you experience an insight, a shift takes place, but *you still have just as much on your plate.* That doesn't magically change. The change is in the way you see what's on your plate. As a result, the sense of there being a problem dissipates. In place of a problem, what you're now left with is a situation.

Charles still had the same number of items on his to-do list after doing ActivInsight, but instead of feeling that he had a problem to struggle with, he had a situation to resolve. That is a crucial shift. As you do more worksheets, you're still going to face situations in life. You will always have challenges and changes to master, but you will be able to see these as situations instead of as problems, and take action from clarity instead of anxiety and frustration.

You don't do this simply by calling problems "situations." The words are not what matter. When you experience anxiety, frustration, sadness, or anger, that tells you that you're seeing a problem, no matter what you might call it. And taking action when you see a problem is likely to lead to further problems. Instead, get out a worksheet and have an insight. Then you'll see the situation more clearly. It may still mean staying up late or working long hours. Some situations require that. But taking action isn't only about the "what." It's also about the "how." And ActivInsight gives you a way to change the how so that you don't just get things done, but you get them done right, with greater intelligence and peace of mind.

That could come in handy, say, when you're trying to navigate a messy divorce. But I'll save that story for the next chapter.

CHAPTER 14

The Myth of Regret

People sometimes say that a life without regret is a life not worth living, but the truth is that regret, like any other form of stress, is not a sign of an adventurous spirit. It's a blind spot hiding something you haven't fully seen yet. The only way to experience regret is to believe that life could or should have happened differently, and as you'll see in the pages that follow, this is always a mistaken notion. Regret lives in the dark. Through insight, we see the truth and let the light in.

I want you to think of one thing that you strongly regret in your life. For this particular worksheet, don't pick something you regret that someone else did. It will be easier for us to go through this together if you find something that *you* did (you can do another worksheet afterward on the other topic). Then, when you have the topic firmly in mind, write on your worksheet the statement overleaf:

1 Write a concise, complete sentence describing something that you experience as stressful. It's helpful to use the words "should" or "shouldn't." (Ex.: "They should listen to me.")

> *I shouldn't have done that.*

_____

_____

If you want to rephrase it so that it's more specific, such as "I shouldn't have married him" or "I shouldn't have invested with them," that's fine. I'm going to use a more general statement, but you can tailor the worksheet to your issue as long as it's close enough that you can follow along.

If it would work better for you to use the word *should* instead of *shouldn't* (you think you should have done something), that's fine, too. But please don't change it to what someone else did, because I want you to focus here on your own personal regrets. What is it that you wish you had or hadn't done in your life?

If you can't think of anything you regret in recent memory, look for something you may have done when you were younger. If you have to go all the way back to elementary school, that's okay as long as it's something you honestly regret and can remember well. But don't just read along. Find something to work on in your life and take the trip with me.

Once you have your regret in mind, how strongly do you feel the belief "I shouldn't have done that" to be true?

2 How strongly do you feel this belief to be true?

0   1   2   3   4   5   6   7   8   9   10

————————————▶ stronger

If you're below a 7, see if you can find something that you regret more strongly, and make sure that you're putting yourself mentally in the place where you feel it most. Not every topic in this book will have a strong charge, but even if this one isn't a high number for you, it's still worth going through because I'm going to introduce a concept that will be useful for other topics as well.

When you think this thought "I shouldn't have done that," how do you feel? Come up with at least three feelings on the list below, adding in words as necessary:

3a How do you *feel* when you believe this?
(Circle below or add your own.)

afraid   abandoned   angry   annoyed   anxious

confused   depressed   desperate   embarrassed

frustrated   helpless   hopeless   hurt   impatient

inadequate   insecure   invisible   jealous   nervous

rejected   resentful   tense   upset   worried

Next, when you're feeling this way, what do you do? Look over the list below carefully and think about how you have treated others and how you have treated yourself as a result of this belief. Each of us expresses regret in slightly different ways, but all of us do something, whether it's drinking, crying, blaming ourselves, getting angry, pulling away. Notice the cause-and-effect relationship in your life, however it appears. Be honest and thorough.

3b How do you *act* when you feel this way?
(Circle below or add your own.)

argue   belittle   blame   bully   complain   cry   drink

eat   escape   fight   find fault with   give up   gossip

insult   interrupt   lose sleep   manipulate   obsess

overwork   pity myself   preach   pretend   procrastinate

shop   shut down   smoke   suffer   withdraw   yell

Step 3 is as dark as ActivInsight gets. Now we start to turn on the lights. What's the negation for the statement "I shouldn't have done that"? Write it on the lines of Step 4.

---

4 Write the negation of your statement from Step 1. In most cases, you also add "In reality" at the beginning and "at this time" or "at that time" at the end.

> *In reality, I should have done that at that time.*

_____

_____

Even for experienced practitioners of ActivInsight, this negation can be a little jarring. Remember that you're not condoning what

216

happened. You're not saying that you want the past to repeat itself. You're only saying that at that time, in reality, there was an intelligence behind it, a logic. That can seem absurd if what you did had negative consequences, in which case you would say that it was definitely not a smart thing to do. To help you see past this, let me introduce a concept I call Relative Peak Intelligence.

Relative Peak Intelligence means that, at any given moment, you're acting with the maximum amount of intelligence you have at your disposal *in that moment.* You're at your peak. This doesn't mean that you're at your *absolute* peak—five minutes later you might know more and make an even more intelligent choice. We're always learning and gaining more experience. But *in the moment* it's the smartest action possible, and so relative to the experience you have at the time, it's your peak. It has to be.

Why? Think about decisions you've made in life, such as who to date, or which job to take, or where to live. Have you ever made a decision in which you said to yourself, "You know what, I could do *this,* or I could do *that. That* would be much smarter, but I'm going to go with the stupider decision and choose *this*"? Look closely and you'll see that you haven't. People do stupid things, but they always think that they're smart at the time, or smart enough.

If you look over even your so-called bad decisions in retrospect, you'll see that, at the moment you made them, they didn't seem so bad. You thought you could get away with it, or that it would work out, or that somehow you would benefit. No one gets married thinking that it's the wrong move. No one places a bet thinking he'll lose. In the single instant during which you make decisions, and relative only to that instant, you make the best decisions you're capable of. That's Relative Peak Intelligence. Watch yourself as you make your next decision, even if it's just what you eat for your next meal, and you'll see that at every point along the way you're doing what you think is best for you based on your own calculations of costs and benefits. Everyone does this.

"But what if I know it's not smart yet I still eat a box of cookies?" I know some people are wondering this, though instead of cookies it may be cigarettes, drugs, gambling, or some other activity. Even when we do something that we "know" we shouldn't—like getting drunk when we're trying to quit drinking or eating sweets when we're trying to be healthier—given where we are on our stress threshold and whether or not we've been restraining ourselves (see chapter 7), that's the smartest choice we're personally capable of at that moment. It doesn't mean the decision is a good one, but it's the best one we can manage at the time. That's why I say the peak intelligence is relative—it's relative to what we are capable of in that moment. Someone who chooses short-term over long-term effects, whether it's cigarettes, drugs, alcohol, food, shopping, or sex, is not yet able in that moment to make a smarter decision. If they were, they would have.

Does saying that you did your best in the past mean that you are free of all consequences? Of course not. Consequences are part of how you learn to make better decisions in the future. They help broaden the list of factors that play into your decision making. But heaping shame and blame upon yourself prevents you from taking in the lesson of your consequences more fully. Instead of judging your past actions or inactions as bad, try to see them—in the moment they happened—as relatively intelligent given your limitations at the time.

To do this, ask yourself, in your particular case, why is it true that in reality you should have done that at that time? Look at the moment as fully and as honestly as you can. What you come up with will differ depending on your situation. Generally speaking, you were unable to see the broader consequences of what you were doing. But why? What were you blinded by? Maybe you were scared, insecure, angry, or greedy. Maybe you were feeling desperate, needy, or wounded. Specify exactly what was going on for you.

Be compassionate as you look for this. We sometimes think that judging our past behaviors harshly is how we prevent ourselves from repeating them or serves as penance of some sort, but this creates an emotional undertow that can pull us backward instead of pushing us forward. So try to go beyond the judgment to see yourself objectively, as if you're looking at someone else who made an unfortunate choice. The more clearly and specifically you can see what was behind that choice, the less likely you are to repeat it, and the more you can integrate the lesson of your own experience. So in Step 5, write down all the ways in which you *should* have done that at that time. What contributed to making it happen?

As an example of what this looks like, let me introduce Lisa. Lisa had gotten married at age twenty-two and was getting a divorce fifteen years later, beating herself up mentally in the process over what this said about her and how it would affect her three young children. Lisa had married someone who, in her words, was "a terrible match for me," and she was "100 percent sure" that she shouldn't have married him. She couldn't even stand to be in the same room as him, and would feel herself frosting over and physically contracting in his presence. When she tried to come up with proof for why she *should* have married him at that time, she drew a blank. "I really shouldn't have," she said matter-of-factly. "It was the biggest mistake of my life."

For a large regret, this is normal. We identify very strongly with the belief, and if we're not going to be happy because of it, at least we have the small satisfaction of knowing that we're right, that we shouldn't have done it, and that we're smart enough to recognize this now. So we're smart, but miserable.

I described the SPIRAL to Lisa, and explained that she could be right (and miserable), or she could have peace of mind. Which did she prefer? She admitted that in her current state of mind she was treating her ex-husband badly in front of their kids, and she didn't want to feel the way she felt. So she pushed herself a little further. How was it true in reality that she *should* have married him at that time? After thinking about it for a few minutes, Lisa confessed that she had liked being the first person in her peer group to get married. It made her feel more mature and one step ahead of her friends. So she wrote that down. That, she said, was the only reason she could come up with.

Then she remembered that, when they were dating, her ex-husband was kind and caring with her younger sister, who has special needs. That had always been a litmus test for Lisa when she introduced people to her family, and he had passed with flying colors. So that also went on the worksheet, because it was another part of why she should have married him at that time—he had passed a very important test. So there were two things. But that was it, she said. There wasn't any other proof.

Except . . . when they had started dating, he had lived downtown and seemed mature and sophisticated and different from the guys she had known in college. So, okay, that was also part of why she should have married him at that time. She had really liked him. "Huh," she said. "I haven't thought about that in a very long time."

In spite of her claims that she was done coming up with proof, with a little coaxing Lisa kept finding more. Anything else that she could remember liking about him at the start, or any factor that might have played a part in her decision to get married, also went on her worksheet. It took time, and it came with some tears, but bit by bit Lisa came up with quite a list. As you read it, notice how she reconstructed the intelligence behind her past actions. She really pushed herself to remember how things were at the time (and not later).

5 Write below all the proof you can find that supports the negation being true in reality at this time (or in the past). Don't rush. Be thorough, using an additional sheet of paper if necessary.

> *In reality, I should have married him at that time because I liked the idea of getting married before my friends and being one step ahead.*

> *In reality, I should have married him at that time because he was kind to my sister, and I remember thinking that he was a good person.*

> *In reality, I should have married him at that time because when we first started dating, we had fun. He lived downtown, was older, and seemed more mature and different from other guys I had dated.*

> *In reality, I should have married him at that time because I had been hurt when my ex-boyfriend got married and I wanted to get married too.*

> *In reality, I should have married him at that time because I wanted to have children right away while I was young.*

> *In reality, I should have married him at that time because he had a strong work ethic, which was important to me, and he was very smart.*

> *In reality, I should have married him at that time because my parents got married young, and I thought that was just what you did.*

> I reality, I should have married him at that time because I thought the early warning signs of our mismatch were normal and that I would be able to resolve them easily.

> In reality, I should have married him at that time because I didn't have any sense of what really makes a marriage work over time. I was twenty-two.

> In reality, I should have married him at that time because seeing clearly who I was then and who he was then, we were actually a good match. It changed later, but if I'm honest I can see that in reality, and at that time, he really was exactly what I wanted.

Can you see how honest Lisa got with herself? These were the reasons why, in reality, she should have married him at that time. She began the worksheet saying that he was a terrible match for her and that this had been the biggest mistake of her life. When she pushed past that and looked at who she and her husband had actually been, she could see something very different, ending with the realization that in fact he had been a very good match *for who she was at the time.* That's Relative Peak Intelligence. It may have changed later, but at the moment she said, "I do," he was the right man to marry—it was not a mistake at all—and what she came up with in Step 5 proves why.

If Lisa's mind then moved to other thoughts (such as "I should have been able to save the marriage" or "We shouldn't have grown apart"), she could do additional worksheets on those topics. As you saw in the chapter on heartbreak, sometimes when you've seen the truth of one belief, another comes up. You want to explore each belief until you see the whole cluster clearly.

So on Step 5 of your worksheet, prove why *in reality* you *should* have done that *at that time.* Do this without blaming yourself or excusing yourself. Try to see it as plainly as you would see a chemistry experiment. To create a chemical reaction, you add together different elements. What were the elements that came together to create the action you regret? What didn't you realize at that time? When you've written them down on your worksheet, take a minute to read them out loud. See if you can come up with any more proof, then continue.

If you were not able to see why you should have done that in reality *at that time,* you may want to spend more time in Step 5 reminding yourself that you're not condoning past behaviors, you're just learning to see them for what they are. If you're stuck and have a friend who does ActivInsight, you might ask him or her for help with the negation. Tell your friend that you have to find ways in which what took place was an expression of intelligence at that time. He or she should be gentle with any suggestions, and you should be as undefended as you can be in exploring possibilities. Our closest friends are often able to help us see inside our blind spots, and we can help them see inside theirs. The online forums at mythofstress.com can also be helpful.

If you *were* able to see why, in reality, you should have done that *at that time,* what feelings come with that? In Lisa's case, she felt compassionate toward herself and her ex-husband for who they had been, and she was relieved that she hadn't actually made a mistake. When she focused her attention squarely on "In reality, I should have married him at that time," she felt a sense of understanding and peace. What do you feel? If you still feel negative emotions, push yourself to go deeper, separating in your mind's eye who you were then from who you are now so you can see your former self with greater compassion. Life is a process of ongoing education. See this clearly, then circle the emotions that come up for you.

6a How do you *feel* when you see the truth of the negation? (Circle below or add your own.)

calm   clear   compassionate   connected   curious

enlightened   enthusiastic   excited   free   grateful

honest   humble   intimate   light   loving   optimistic

peaceful   playful   relaxed   relieved   serene

supportive   tolerant   truthful   understanding

Then, how might you act when you feel this way? Lisa could envision spending time with her ex-husband without feeling angry and resentful. That doesn't mean that she wanted to be married to him again. But once she saw that, in reality, she hadn't made a mistake and that he had once been the man she wanted to marry, she stopped blaming him. She also saw her present needs even more clearly and began dating someone who met them.

When you see that you should have done what you did, what actions could follow for you? How would your behaviors change? Look over Step 6b and see what you can come up with.

6b What *actions* might come from this? (Circle below or add your own.)

accept   apologize   approach   be honest   breathe

clarify   communicate   contribute   delegate   exercise

explore   focus   follow through   forgive   give thanks

listen   make amends   network   open up   participate

prioritize   reach out   share   speak up   support

Finally, let's return to your original statement: "I shouldn't have done that." Reviewing your list in Step 5, and keeping Relative Peak Intelligence in mind, how true is that in reality? Lisa gave it a 2.5, circling 2 and 3. What number feels right to you?

7 Read your original statement again. How strongly do you feel this belief to be true now?

0   1   2   3   4   5   6   7   8   9   10

weaker ⟵————————

Did you go down in points from Step 1? And are you dropping more points now than in earlier worksheets? If so, good work. That means the steps are getting clearer.

Relative Peak Intelligence can be very helpful in dismantling a wide range of stressful beliefs. You'll often hear people saying things such as "I could have done better," especially in sports. But when someone misses a free throw in a championship game, or shanks a golf ball in a playoff, or accidentally lets a baseball go through his legs in the World Series, in that moment that person was acting as intelligently as he possibly could. He wasn't saying, "Maybe I'll reduce my concentration and blow this one." Hundreds of muscles have to coordinate perfectly in order to pull off these acts of physical intelligence, and athletes have thousands of distracting stimuli to tune out. Sometimes we don't do this as well as at other times, and sometimes that lapse happens close to the end of the game, but we were still operating at our relative peak. That doesn't mean we can't do better in the future, but thinking that we could have done better *in the past* is an exercise in masochism and futility, because it's wrong. We could not have. Not at that time. And if you can't see this, it's worth getting out a work-sheet to prove it.

The myth of regret shows up widely throughout our culture. In the classic movie *On the Waterfront,* Marlon Brando's character, Terry Malloy, regrets having taken a dive in the boxing ring years earlier so that his brother Charley could collect on some bets. "I coulda been a contender," he says wistfully. "I coulda been some-body." But in reality, could Terry have been a contender at that time? Why not? You can watch the movie to find out for your-self, but part of the proof involves his inability to stand up to his brother at that time, the extra money he made, and the likely belief that he would get another chance. Brando's line has become iconic because it captures the regret that so many people feel. But that doesn't make it true.

Regret is one of the most concentrated forms of counterfactual thinking. Instead of simply dramatizing regret, we can transcend it. We may tell ourselves and one another that what happened could have happened differently, but in reality the only thing that could have happened is what actually did happen. There is great variability in our future, but none in our past. Why not? Because it happened already.

So when your neocortex spins a story about how things could or should have happened another way, bring yourself back to the real world. Get out a worksheet and see exactly why what happened happened, and why it *had* to happen that way at that time. That's how you can learn from the past without shame and guilt. Then maybe people will start to say that a life without regret is a wise and happy life indeed.

CHAPTER 15

The Myth of Discrimination

Aren't we beyond this already? It's the twenty-first century. People shouldn't discriminate."

I was leading an ActivInsight workshop at a gay and lesbian community center, and I wanted to know what the participants experienced as stressful. The first answers were the same answers I hear everywhere—money, success, relationships, body image, family conflict. But then the subject of discrimination came up. A gentleman named Larry held the floor.

"It's the same fight every time," Larry continued. "Black rights. Women's rights. Why does it have to be such a long and bitter struggle? Don't they see that they're going to lose? People should just recognize that we're all equal and have equal rights, and be done with it. Honestly, sometimes it makes me ashamed to be human."

There were nods around the room. The topic obviously struck a nerve.

"Okay," I said. "So let's use that belief on our worksheet."

"Which belief?" Larry asked. "I have a lot."

Everyone laughed.

"We're going to work on 'They shouldn't discriminate.'"

When I teach ActivInsight to a group, I look for beliefs that resonate for the majority of people in the room. I usually do this by having participants fill out an online survey where they can rate a variety of beliefs, and then in the session we focus on the most popular choices. In this case, however, we hadn't done a survey and I didn't know which beliefs the participants were stressed-out over, so I found out the low-tech way.

In another part of the country, the consensus might have been very different—something along the lines of "Gay people shouldn't seek the right to marry." That would have been a good worksheet topic as well. ActivInsight doesn't have a political agenda. It can be used by anyone on anything stressful. (And if you want to work through the belief on gay marriage, it's online at mythofstress.com.)

To get started on the topic of discrimination, think of someone who you think should not discriminate. The worksheet below focuses on sexual discrimination, but if your issue is with another form of discrimination (gender, race, culture, religion, physical ability, etc.), move it in that direction. Personalizing it to "The management committee shouldn't discriminate against women" or "White people shouldn't discriminate against blacks" is encouraged. This is your worksheet. Get out of it what you can.

On the lines of Step 1, write:

1 Write a concise, complete sentence describing something that you experience as stressful. It's helpful to use the words "should" or "shouldn't." (Ex.: "They should listen to me.")

> *They shouldn't discriminate.*

_____

_____

In Step 2, bring the emotions of this to the surface of your mind by picturing these people in the act of discrimination. What number would you circle?

"Why does it only go to 10?" Larry asked, tongue in cheek. We're looking for 7s and higher. If you're below a 7, make sure you're working on the strongest experience of discrimination you can.

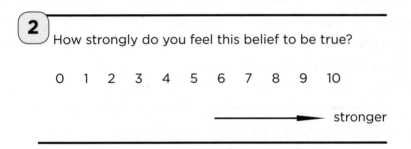

2 How strongly do you feel this belief to be true?

0   1   2   3   4   5   6   7   8   9   10

———————————▶ stronger

Next, when you think this thought, "They shouldn't discriminate," and you see discrimination in the world, how do you feel?

People around the room contributed their feelings: angry, depressed, frustrated, hurt, resentful, tense, upset. Find at least three feelings on your worksheet, but circle as many as ring true, and write in any others that come to mind.

3a How do you *feel* when you believe this?
(Circle below or add your own.)

afraid   abandoned   angry   annoyed   anxious

confused   depressed   desperate   embarrassed

frustrated   helpless   hopeless   hurt   impatient

inadequate   insecure   invisible   jealous   nervous

rejected   resentful   tense   upset   worried

In Step 3b, when you feel this way, note how you act. Do you take this out on anyone? How does this affect your relationships or your job? How does it affect the way you treat your body? How do you treat people who discriminate? What do you do?

"This may be hard for you to believe," Larry said, "but I've been known to complain."

The rest of the participants volunteered more behaviors: Blame. Lose sleep. Pity myself. Give up hope. Curse. Drink. Avoid others. Segregate. Preach. Suffer. Smoke. Judge.

Look over the list and think about what actions arise in your life, being as honest as you can be.

3b How do you *act* when you feel this way?
(Circle below or add your own.)

argue	belittle	blame	bully	complain	cry	drink
eat	escape	fight	find fault with	give up		gossip
insult	interrupt	lose sleep	manipulate	obsess		
overwork	pity myself	preach	pretend	procrastinate		
shop	shut down	smoke	suffer	withdraw	yell	

In Step 4, what's the negation for "They shouldn't discriminate"? Add it to your worksheet.

4 Write the negation of your statement from Step 1. In most cases, you also add "In reality" at the beginning and "at this time" or "at that time" at the end.

> *In reality, they should discriminate at this time.*

_____

_____

_____

"I don't think I can write that," Larry said. "It goes against every cell in my body. Why would I want to believe that?"

"Keep in mind," I said, "that this statement isn't saying that we want people to discriminate, or that we like discrimination, or that we encourage discrimination. We're not saying that they should discriminate more, or even that they should discriminate tomorrow. We're using 'should' to point just to this moment so we can see it more clearly, and maybe by doing that, shift how we feel and how we act in the world. We're not condoning discrimination. We're investigating it. What is this thing called discrimination? How can we address it if we don't even understand it?"

"I do understand it." Larry said. "It's bigotry."

"Let's say you're right," I said, "Discrimination is bigotry. We can also call it prejudice. We can call it hate, or ignorance, or a dozen other words. But do you see that we're just moving sideways when we do this? We're not really going deeper. Some people may not want to go deeper. They just want to be right, and they're done. But if you're interested in living with less stress, it may be that we need to head in a slightly different direction. Are you open to seeing where this leads?"

I explained the ActivInsight SPIRAL and then repeated the question, waiting for a response. Sometimes the negations can seem too great a leap. People have died because of discrimination. These thoughts can be highly charged. And I'm aware that many people have no interest in questioning their most stressful beliefs. They want the world to change and don't see how their own thoughts play a part. I don't work with these people, simply because ActivInsight doesn't work with these people. I can coach, I can push a little and help guide, but someone has to be willing to question their own beliefs if they want to have an insight. Part of why I offer workshops at places like this gay and lesbian center is that, in my experience, the people who attend (gay or straight) are generally open-minded. But that's not always the case.

"Yeah, I guess I'm open," Larry said, writing the negation on his worksheet. "I don't like it, but it won't kill me to do this exercise."

I wasn't so sure about that. The "me" that starts a worksheet is not the "me" who finishes it. But I held my tongue.

Next, in Step 5, you prove the negation. Why is it true that "In reality, they should discriminate at this time"? See what you can come up with on your own before going further.

Below is the proof we came up with in that room. Read it through and use it to help prove the negation on your worksheet.

In reality, they should discriminate at this time because they were taught to think discriminatory thoughts.

It's always helpful to begin with the most obvious proof. One way to find this is to temporarily take out the word *should* and replace it with, in this case, *do,* making the negation read, "In reality, people *do* discriminate at this time," and then ask why that is. I call this "flattening the should." One obvious reason people *do* discriminate at this time is because they were taught to think discriminatory thoughts.

We begin life without the ability to discriminate at all. We don't even know where we end and other people begin. This is something we learn. Then we learn the names of everyday objects and people around us. We learn numbers and letters. And, in some homes, formally or informally, we learn discrimination. It's how some of us were taught to think, and it became part of our worldview. You may not like it, you may wish this didn't happen, but it's reality, and so it forms part of why they should discriminate at this time. If you can see that this is true, take a deep breath, write it down, and continue.

In reality, they should discriminate at this time because they believe that our differences matter.

Even though the human species shares most traits (two eyes, two ears, etc.), we each look a little bit different, and every culture invests some of these differences with meaning. The color of your skin, the kind of reproductive organs you have, whether or not the people you find attractive have similar reproductive organs—these are a few of the differences that some people consider meaningful at this time, differences that supposedly say something about you. Whether or not this is true in *your* mind, in *their* mind these differences are considered important, and so this is part of why, in reality, they should discriminate at this time. Can you see this? If so, add it to your worksheet, then continue.

In reality, they should discriminate at this time because they want things to remain a certain way, and I seem to threaten that. (Specify how.)

Discrimination takes place when one group has favored status. Maybe they have more money. Maybe they have more power to make decisions. But in some way they have established themselves as dominant, and you seem to threaten that. Consequently, they *should* discriminate against you at this time because, consciously or not, they want to maintain their favored status, and you challenge that in some way. If that seems true in your case, you would write it on your worksheet. If you can specify how you challenge them and what they are afraid of, add that as well, then continue to the next proof.

In reality, they should discriminate at this time because they have never had an experience proving their beliefs to be wrong.

This is another obvious proof that we often overlook. If someone who has learned to discriminate does *not* have an experience that challenges his beliefs, what happens? Nothing. That's the law of inertia. Without any outside force to change it, an object in motion stays in motion, and an object at rest stays at rest. So part of why they should discriminate at this time is that they have never had an experience proving their beliefs to be wrong. *You* may have had experiences like this, but they haven't yet. They have never been exposed to someone or something (a book, a movie, a documentary, a conversation) that successfully challenged their perspective and changed their point of view. Maybe they live in seclusion. Maybe they are surrounded by people who think the same way they do. That doesn't mean that they won't change in the future, but if it's the way things are now (and if they are discriminating against you, it is), you want to see this. That's part of why they discriminate against you at this time. If that seems true to you, add that to your list and continue.

In reality, they should discriminate at this time because they don't see what they're doing as discrimination. (Specify why not.)

This takes a little more reflection to see, but it reveals the myth of discrimination for what it is. There is no such thing as discrimination in someone's own experience. If person A discriminates against person B, A doesn't think he is discriminating. He thinks he's upholding a valuable tradition. That's not discrimination—it's moral duty. To someone looking from the outside, of course, A's action may be patently discriminatory. But part of why it took place, and part of why they should discriminate against you at this time, is because they don't see what they're doing as discrimination.

In many workplaces, for example, management promotes the brightest people to leadership positions. This may seem nondiscriminatory because they're promoting on the basis of intelligence and talent. But if certain minorities were denied equal educational opportunities in the past, those minorities wouldn't have had the same chances to develop their intelligence and talent. This is why discriminatory practices from the past result in underrepresentation today, which leads to further discrimination in the future (the law of inertia again) unless special programs to foster minority talent are put in place. The people making decisions based on intelligence or performance may have no idea that they're acting in a discriminatory fashion. They may think they're just doing what's best, and as a result short-term fairness becomes long-term inequality.

Obviously this isn't always the case. Sometimes discrimination is intentional and everyone knows it. But if you can see ways in which the person or group you're writing about may not be fully aware that their actions toward you are discriminatory, add that to your worksheet and specify why not. If this doesn't apply to your situation, skip it and move on to the next suggestion.

In reality, they should discriminate at this time because the modern human brain slips easily into rigid categorization.

Let's return to the gray, wrinkled neocortex, home of the brain's enormous capacity for abstract thought. Thanks to the neocortex, we learn to see the world as containing separate things: hand, foot,

Mommy, Daddy, bottle. This generally is followed by individualization (me, you, them), followed when we're a little older by identification with groups, such as family, cliques in school, sports teams, religious groups, cultures, and nations. Other animals organize into groups, but no other animal on Earth categorizes to the extent of Homo sapiens. (See? We've even come up with a whole system of categorization.)

The construction of the human mind predisposes us to categorization and adherence to these categories (male, female, straight, gay, white, black . . .). Consequently, part of why they should discriminate at this time is that they are not a chimpanzee, or a tree squirrel, or a lichen. They are a human being, born with the tendency to think in categories, to discriminate based on those categories, and to resist seeing beyond those categories. Some people do see beyond them, of course, but apparently not the people you're working on, so this goes on your list. And that brings up the next suggestion.

In reality, they should discriminate at this time because they couldn't be any more open-minded given their life experiences so far (Relative Peak Intelligence).

We often say things such as "They should have known better" or "They didn't have to act that way" when we refer to episodes of discrimination. But the reality is that they should *not* have known better at that time given the life they have had, and so they *did* have to act that way.

This is another example of Relative Peak Intelligence. When we think people could have been more open-minded, it breeds anger and resentment inside us. These are signs that our own mind has closed itself off and contracted into a lie. Even the most racist, sexist, and prejudiced people are, *in their minds,* holding on to valid beliefs, and so they are doing their best. They were acting their most open-minded given where they were coming from. That can be a tough one to wrap your mind around, but if you can see this as true, add it to your worksheet, then continue.

In reality, they should discriminate at this time because people in my position in the past have either polarized matters further or given up. (Specify who, if you can.)

You are not the first person to think the thought "People shouldn't discriminate." You're probably not even the first person in your particular situation, with this particular person or people. Did those who came before you succeed in helping change the situation? Apparently not. So part of why they should discriminate at this time is that anyone in your position in the past either polarized matters further or gave up. That's not a criticism of those past people. It's just a fact. If it applies in your case, write it on your worksheet, and if you can, specify who these people were. Then continue to the final suggestion.

In reality, they should discriminate at this time because I have written them off as incapable of change. (Specify how.)

The last part of Step 5 involves seeing your part. Remember that their part may be 99 percent of the problem and your part 1 percent, but you still have to find that 1 percent because otherwise you're not taking responsibility for your share.

How have you written off the people whom you're writing about? The participants in the workshop came up with the following: "I have made fun of them. I have dismissed them as idiots, incapable of change. I have demonized them. I tell myself that I don't know these people, when really they must live and work around me. I spend my energy complaining or blaming them instead of thinking of ways to engage them in dialogue, or even just getting to know them. I have made no effort to understand them but I complain that they don't understand me."

That last step of proving the negation is always humbling. It's a hard look straight in the mirror. See if you can come up with more proof on your worksheet, then read your answers to Step 5 out loud:

---

5 Write below all the proof you can find that supports the negation being true in reality at this time (or in the past). Don't rush. Be thorough, using an additional sheet of paper if necessary.

> *In reality, they should discriminate at this time because they were taught to think discriminatory thoughts.*

> *In reality, they should discriminate at this time because they believe that our differences matter.*

> *In reality, they should discriminate at this time because they want things to remain a certain way, and I seem to threaten that. (Specify how.)*

> *In reality, they should discriminate at this time because they have never had an experience proving their beliefs to be wrong.*

> *In reality, they should discriminate at this time because they don't see what they're doing as discrimination. (Specify why not.)*

> *In reality, they should discriminate at this time because the modern human brain slips easily into rigid categorization.*

> *In reality, they should discriminate at this time because they couldn't be any more open-minded given their life experiences so far (Relative Peak Intelligence).*

> *In reality, they should discriminate at this time because people in my position in the past have either polarized matters further or given up. (Specify who, if you can.)*

> *In reality, they should discriminate at this time because I have written them off as incapable of change. (Specify how.)*

I asked Larry to read the list out loud to the room. He did. I then asked him how he felt.

"I'll be honest," he said. "For those first two, I felt really angry, and I still didn't get what this was about. But then when we kept going, I started to get it. You're not saying that people should discriminate, as in, this is a good activity to engage in. You're saying that people should discriminate, as in, that's what some people on Earth do at this moment. And when I got that, it made sense to me. People should discriminate right now, because, duh, that's how they woke up this morning."

"Right," I said, admiring Larry's way of putting it. "And how does that feel, seeing things that way?"

"I feel . . ." Larry thought for a moment. "I don't know what the word is. Wiser, maybe. And broader, like my vision has expanded somehow. And maybe even a teensy bit understanding. I don't think I'm ready to be all kumbaya about this, but I do feel different."

We laughed. I asked the rest of the participants to find three feelings on their worksheets in Step 6a. Do the same now on your worksheet.

6a How do you **feel** when you see the truth of the negation? (Circle below or add your own.)

calm   clear   compassionate   connected   curious
enlightened   enthusiastic   excited   free   grateful
honest   humble   intimate   light   loving   optimistic
peaceful   playful   relaxed   relieved   serene
supportive   tolerant   truthful   understanding

In Step 6b, when you feel the way you've just indicated, how might you act? I asked Larry.

"I'm not sure how I would act. I do feel like I see things differently," he said. "Like now instead of 'them' in my mind being an unthinking evil horde, they're more like children who have simply been taught divisive beliefs. I don't know what I would do with that. I'm not moving to Utah."

People in the room laughed. "Can I ask you a question?" I asked.

"Please."

"I realize that you were joking, but can you see any way in which imagining that taking action requires your moving to Utah could be another part of why they should discriminate at this time?"

"Ah," Larry said, smiling. "Boy, you don't give us an inch, do you? Okay, yes. I can see that. I do jump to extremes. And I'm probably leaping over things I could do that might make a difference without my becoming Mormon, and making some other broad assumptions. I'll think about that. Thank you."

Seeing that they should discriminate at this time doesn't mean that you adopt their point of view, or that you accept their discrimination and move on. As I mentioned in the beginning of the book, this is called ActivInsight for two reasons: First, it turns insight into an active, step-by-step process. And second, it gives you action steps to follow. When you have an insight and see things more honestly, take action from that greater wisdom. What can you do? What steps, large or small, might help create change on both sides of the aisle?

People in that room talked about reaching out, looking for ways to steer the debate in a more productive direction, being less divisive themselves, listening better to the other side, and attempting to communicate their own position with less hostility in a way that others might actually hear. Seeing the truth is not about being passive. In some cases, it may mean you file a lawsuit. But even this can be done calmly and without stress when your eyes are open and your vision is clear.

Look over the list in Step 6b and see what actions you come up with when you see that "In reality, they should discriminate at this time."

6b What *actions* might come from this?
(Circle below or add your own.)

accept	apologize	approach	be honest	breathe
clarify	communicate	contribute	delegate	exercise
explore	focus	follow through	forgive	give thanks
listen	make amends	network	open up	participate
prioritize	reach out	share	speak up	support

Finally, in Step 7, how strongly do you believe the original statement, "They shouldn't discriminate," to be true now?

The men and women in that room ranged between 0 and 5 (Larry was a 4). How true is it to you?

7 Read your original statement again. How strongly do you feel this belief to be true now?

0   1   2   3   4   5   6   7   8   9   10

weaker ⟵————————

Good job completing another worksheet. Some people drop five or more points on this and feel their head ending up in a very different place. But even if you didn't, if you reflected on each step sincerely and read through the suggestions to see if they were true for you, you covered a lot of ground.

Whenever discrimination happens, it *should* happen. Not for the rest of time, but just *at that moment,* because there are underlying causes. It's like a lake filled by underground streams. As long as those streams are still flowing, that lake should exist. Denying it and saying that the lake shouldn't exist would be insane. The streams are right there, filling it. Similarly, saying "discrimination shouldn't happen" when it still does is an act of insanity. It's a form of ignorance and denial that blinds you to the underlying causes you desperately need to see. Seeing that discrimination *should* happen when it does (not before or after) lifts the mind out of this ignorance and enables it to play a new part. You change, so you can consider new ways to help others change.

This can be called psychological or spiritual growth, but really it would be more correct to call it shrinkage. By challenging your own beliefs, you're left with less of yourself, not more. And as a result of this shrinking, there's more space within you for compassion, empathy, creativity, and dialogue. That's the subtractive power of insight.

The next chapter is the last worksheet we're going to do together in this book. It's the black diamond ski run I mentioned when we first began. If you have dropped more than five points on one or more of these last three worksheets, and especially if you've had the mind-opening feeling of "Aha" that comes with insight, you're ready. But what if you haven't?

The beautiful thing about a book, as opposed to a live workshop, is that you can go back and reread chapters, do more worksheets, and solidify the basic principles. You might do another worksheet on any of the earlier chapters. You could also try a completely new topic on your own, such as "They should listen to me" or "They should appreciate me more" (make sure you look for your part in Step 5).

Then, when you feel ready, tighten your bindings and meet me at the chairlift for chapter 16. We've got some expert skiing to do.

CHAPTER 16

The Myth of Dying Too Soon

In chapter 2, I mentioned that we were going to work through a range of issues together, starting like beginning skiers do with an easy trail and working our way through intermediate topics up to a black diamond. This chapter, the final worksheet we'll do together in this book, is the black diamond.

Obviously this is not really skiing, and the comparison only goes so far. My point is only that ActivInsight, like any skill, can be difficult at first but gets easier with practice so that, when you really do it well, it becomes fun. That may sound odd. How can working on your problems be fun? In fact, mental well-being can be just as enjoyable a pursuit as physical well-being. When you experience stress, taking a few minutes to do an ActivInsight worksheet very quickly gets things flowing again and leaves you clear-headed and energized.

That said, if you skipped here out of curiosity, I invite you to go back and read the previous chapters before continuing. The only time that people misinterpret ActivInsight is when they try to use it without really understanding it. The topics in part 2 incrementally build a skill set that you'll need here. If you don't understand what I mean by counterfactual thinking, subtractive versus additive processes, Relative Peak Intelligence, and using the word *should* to point to reality instead of your imagination, review the earlier chapters so these concepts are clear.

Ideally, you'd have experienced a significant point drop by now, having started at 8, 9, or 10 and ended at 3 or lower on a single worksheet. If you are still dropping only one or two points, I have a suggestion. Skip this chapter for now and go to the appendix, where I answer commonly asked questions about ActivInsight and clarify some of the gray areas. It sometimes happens that a single lingering concern, once resolved, enables someone to experience this process very differently. Then revisit the earlier chapters again and see if they make more sense. When you're consistently dropping five or more points, come back and meet me here.

I'm not saying this to frighten you off. I'm saying it because in this chapter I'm going to show you what ActivInsight looks like when you approach a big issue and put your mind's full creative energy into it. For someone who is not ready it will be too much. For someone who *is* ready, though, it can be quite a trip.

To start with a painful thought that seems undeniably true and watch it become less and less true as you apply yourself is astounding. To finally break through an issue that you had struggled with for weeks, months, or years is enlightening. To realize that, no matter what happens in your life—*no matter what happens in your life*—you can handle it because you know how to handle your own thoughts is empowering. And to see mental fitness as something you can provide for yourself, just like physical fitness, is nothing short of revolutionary.

As exciting as this may be in theory, the real excitement comes from practice, and we have one more exercise to practice on together here. The statement that we're going to work on now is "He shouldn't have died." I want you to think of someone in your life who you believe died too soon. If no one close to you has passed away, you can work on someone in the public eye whose death had an impact on you. But don't just read this chapter as a spectator. Get a pen, print a worksheet, and experience it for yourself.

Over the course of this book, I've shared a number of different people's stories so that you had someone to relate to as you went through your worksheet. Since this was the topic that initially catalyzed my interest in self-help, in this chapter I'm going to share my own experiences. For me, this topic relates most strongly to three people—my father, who died of a heart attack at the age of sixty-one; my half sister, who died in a car accident at the age of three; and my older half brother, who took his own life at the age of thirty-seven, twelve years after our father died. I'll say more about these events as we go forward.

Think of the person who you think shouldn't have died, and on the lines of Step 1, write the following:

1 Write a concise, complete sentence describing something that you experience as stressful. It's helpful to use the words "should" or "shouldn't." (Ex.: "They should listen to me.")

> *They shouldn't have died.*

_____

_____

You can change it to "He," "She," "John," "My daughter," or whatever is right for you, but please keep the rest of the sentence the same.

Then, in Step 2, you know what to do. Put yourself mentally in the place where you most strongly believe this thought. Imagine their lives cut short and the things they'll never get to experience. From that place, what number would you rate this belief? It was a 10 for me. Pick the right number for you.

2 How strongly do you feel this belief to be true?

0   1   2   3   4   5   6   7   8   9   10

—————————▶ stronger

Next, when you think this thought, how do you feel? Let yourself really feel it. If tears come up, let them come. As you experience whatever feelings arise, slowly look over the list in 3a. How do you feel when you believe the thought "They shouldn't have died"? I circled *depressed, helpless,* and *upset,* and wrote in *empty.* Circle the words that feel accurate to you, and add any emotions that aren't on the list.

3a How do you *feel* when you believe this?
(Circle below or add your own.)

afraid   abandoned   angry   annoyed   anxious

confused   depressed   desperate   embarrassed

frustrated   helpless   hopeless   hurt   impatient

inadequate   insecure   invisible   jealous   nervous

rejected   resentful   tense   upset   worried

In Step 3b, what happens in your life when you feel this way? How do you act?

When I was a teenager and felt sad about my father's death, for example, I would cry, pity myself, and suffer. But in addition to that, I also stopped caring about my grades in school. After my little sister died, I became paranoid that other people close to me were going to die. I saw my friends as naïve. And I questioned the existence of a higher power that makes decisions about life and death.

These may not be what someone would call healthy reactions, but they were my reactions, and when I fill out a worksheet I want to be as honest as I can be. So in addition to the behaviors listed in 3b on the worksheet, I would write in these other ones. Then, looking at Steps 1 through 3, I can see the cause-and-effect relationship between my original thought ("They shouldn't have died"), the feelings that followed, and the resulting behaviors. It doesn't have to be a pretty picture. It just has to be real.

How do you act when you think this thought and feel the way you just wrote down?

3b How do you **act** when you feel this way?
(Circle below or add your own.)

argue   belittle   blame   bully   complain   cry   drink

eat   escape   fight   find fault with   give up   gossip

insult   interrupt   lose sleep   manipulate   obsess

overwork   pity myself   preach   pretend   procrastinate

shop   shut down   smoke   suffer   withdraw   yell

Next, we move to Step 4. What's the negation for "They shouldn't have died"? Make sure you keep breathing as you write it on your worksheet.

4 Write the negation of your statement from Step 1. In most cases, you also add "In reality" at the beginning and "at this time" or "at that time" at the end.

> *In reality, they should have died at that time.*

_____

_____

Before we attempt Step 5, remind yourself that we're not condoning their death. "Should" in ActivInsight has nothing to do with what you want to happen. Should is a pure reflection of life. Should is. You don't have to like it. You don't have to accept it. But when you resist it, you suffer because your mind has pulled away from life itself. This pulling away is the pain that you feel, not their loss, though this seems so hard to believe. For years I was sure that what I felt was the loss of my family members. It never crossed my mind that my sense of loss was produced through my own thought patterns. But this isn't hard to demonstrate.

People are dying right now all around the world, yet you don't feel any sense of loss at all until you have a thought about it. Remember, What You Think Is What You Feel. These thoughts may seem like they will be painful forever (remember that gentleman who told me my pain would last for the rest of my life?), but they don't have to be.

The less you see your loved one's death as an aberration, the less pain you will experience. But how do you get there without pretending? You have to bring the mind back to the real world and close the gap. It's like suturing a wound, stitch by stitch, with each proof of the negation. This means asking yourself why it's true that, in reality, they should have died at that time. Can you come up with any possible reason this could be true?

The "should" on this one may still feel harsh. For many people, this is the hardest topic in this book (for some it's the hardest topic they could possibly do), and you may feel resistance as your mind reflexively contracts around the belief that they *shouldn't* have died. This is natural. But it also leaves you deeply mired in sadness and self-pity, so we're going to press further and look for proof of the negation.

To get things started, we can "flatten the should." Putting the concept of "should" aside for the moment, why is it true that they *did* die? One reason is, they were not superhuman or immortal. That's part of why they died at that time, so it's part of why they *should* have died at that time, because "should" in ActivInsight reflects reality, not imagination. As you write down this proof on your worksheet, remind yourself that this doesn't in any way condone their death or excuse anyone involved. Of course you wish that they hadn't died. But given that they did, our focus now is not on them but on you and your ability to find peace with this. Look for ways in which it's true that, in reality, given the circumstances, they should have died at that time, and write what you find. Then continue to the paragraph below and I'll make some additional suggestions.

The suggestions below are drawn from my own experience and my desire to understand the truth, regardless of what others said was true. This journey took place over years but is presented here in just a few pages. Go slowly, and if any of these suggestions rings true for you, add it to your worksheet. If it gives you an idea for something else, then add that, but make sure you do this on paper and not in your head. It's always important to write the proofs for the negation on paper.

In reality, they should have died at that time because they were not immortal.

This is a good place to start. I loved my father, and I may have never thought about his death before he died, but the reality is, he was human. The same is true for my little sister, my older brother, and the person you're working on. This is the very first step in seeing that in reality they should have died at that time. We can then build on this in the next proof.

In reality, they should have died at that time because the human body is fragile.

You may avoid thinking about the fragility of the human body, but it's worth noting that not all bodies are made this way. An ant can fall hundreds of feet through the air and land without a scratch. You can squeeze a flea hard between your fingers and yet it springs away, unscathed. These creatures have little bodies with tough external skeletons. Humans, however, are comparatively large and soft, and as a result we are very vulnerable to damage.

Sometimes this damage is inflicted from the outside, as in the case of my little sister. Sometimes it happens invisibly from the inside, as with my father. Sometimes it's self-inflicted, as with my brother. But part of why we die is simply because of how we're made. If you can see that, and can recognize it as part of why, in reality, they should have died at that time, write it on your worksheet, take it in for a moment, then go on to the next suggestion.

In reality, they should have died at that time because our medical knowledge is still very limited.

This proof is not a condemnation of the current medical system, nor is it a reason to feel hopeless or fatalistic. It's simply the way things are. We can save countless people now that we couldn't save fifty years ago, and the same will be said in fifty years of people who die today, whether it's from disease, accidents, or depression. But progress takes time, and right now the state of our medical knowledge—as advanced as it may be in many areas—is still very limited. If you can see that this is also part of why, in reality at this time, they should have died, add it to your worksheet, take it in for a moment, then continue.

In reality, they should have died at that time because their body reached a definite point beyond which it could not sustain life.

This is a slightly stronger restatement of the first two proofs. It's helpful to go further into this because otherwise many of us tend to think magically, saying things such as "They had so much life left in them." But the reality is that they had exactly as much life as they had, with none left over. Their body reached a point where it could no longer sustain itself. This is why they died.

The forces and constraints that determine life and death for the trillions of life forms on this planet are not going to be magically suspended so that people I love can live a little longer, but this is in effect what I was demanding when I said they should not have died. When I realized this, I saw that when someone dies—for whatever reason—their body could not live even one minute longer. Instead of focusing then on their death as a violation of the order of things, I took one step closer to seeing that, in fact, their death was a part of the order of things. It was bounded by the laws of physiology that describe how life works for all of us. Death is what takes place when life can no longer be sustained, and their body—no matter how it got there—reached a point where life could no longer be sustained. That's part of why they should have died at that time. If you can see this, add the proof above to your worksheet and continue to the next suggestion.

In reality, they should have died at that time because life makes no promises.

This one may be a little harder to land on, so let's go slowly.

Most of us believe that life is supposed to look a certain way. We're supposed to have a happy childhood, do well in school, get a good job, fall in love, have a family, and then spend the rest of our lives balancing professional accomplishments with a rich and fulfilling family life, while also finding time to help others and make a difference in the world. And then finally, at the end of our loving, healthy, successful, respected, philanthropic, and fulfilling life, we're supposed to die quickly and painlessly at a ripe old age, feeling at peace that our work here is done. Whether or not we admit it, that's how most of us subconsciously believe life is supposed to look. That's the gold standard we measure ourselves by.

So when someone falls far short of this, when someone dies at a much younger age than they're "supposed" to, or when they die in an accident or take their own life, it seems like a crime, as if the future they were due and the accomplishments they had yet to achieve were violently stolen from them. But life makes no promises. Life guarantees us nothing. Life has no agenda, and no plan. In the case of someone dying "too soon," it's the counterfactual mind—not life—that invents the concept of a future, and it's the counterfactual mind—not life—that then bewails the theft of its own creation, pointing the finger at life for a crime that never took place at all.

Life never said that people don't die young. In fact, life has always been very clear that they do. From the beginning of time, people have died young, and in every possible way: fire, murder, accident, war, suicide, disease, earthquake, flood. They've died in the water, they've died in the air, and they've died on land. Everyone who ever walked this Earth before our time has died or will, many of them young, and almost none of them in the way and at the moment they anticipated. Yet the counterfactual mind clings stubbornly to the belief that life and death are supposed to happen in a certain way, and that this person died "too soon." But there is no "too soon" in life. There is just the way things are.

Eventually, tired of the pain of believing that my family members shouldn't have died, I asked myself a question I had never asked myself before: who is more qualified to teach me the truth about life, other people and their beliefs, or life itself? When I believed that my loved ones shouldn't have died, I hurt, and to some degree I saw their lives as failed efforts. But when I began to take life at face value, without the idea that it had somehow gotten itself wrong, I could see something else. In recognizing that life makes no promises except to be exactly what it is, I could see what it is, and I could appreciate what it is, instead of comparing it violently to what it isn't.

This changed how I felt and how I saw my loved ones. Before, I would think of my father or one of my siblings and the image was followed immediately by the belief that what had happened to them was terrible, they had been denied what they were owed, a grave act of injustice had been committed. Not only did this fill me with anger and sadness, but also it made their lives seem tarnished somehow.

Yet when I realized the truth about what took place and could see that *life makes no promises,* it's as if the memories were purified and were no longer overshadowed by my own confusion. My family members hadn't been cheated of anything. They had simply died. And seeing this, I could stop focusing on their deaths, and I could see their lives again. I could remember them with peace, and even happiness. I could see them as entirely successful as defined by their own lives, not by my fantasies.

Recognizing that life makes no promises may sound depressing at first, but it opens you up to something beautiful and rarely seen. It's as if you're taking the ability to appreciate diversity in various areas of life and you're extending this to life itself, freeing yourself from the limiting belief that what a complete life looks like and how it ends has to appear a certain way. That's how flexible and unlimited reality itself is. Can you be flexible and unlimited enough in your thinking to see it?

If you can, then add to your worksheet that, in reality, they should have died at that time because life makes no promises except to be itself. Try to see this not as condemnatory, but as a sign of integrity. Should is. You can argue with it for your entire life, but still, should is. You're arguing with the way of the world.

If your loved one died through sudden injury or by their own hand, you may still think that they could have avoided this, that it really didn't have to happen. But could it have *not* happened? Let's look at this more closely in the next proof.

In reality, they should have died at that time because it could not have happened another way.

It seems there are so many ways in which their death didn't have to happen. In the case of someone who died by disease, they could have eaten differently, for example, or exercised more, or not smoked, or seen a different doctor. But can you see that, in reality, given who they were and how they lived their life, none of this is true? In each moment, they did the best they could. They gave up whatever they could give up, they changed whatever they could change. They made every choice to the best of their ability. The same was true of their doctors, or anyone else in a decision-making capacity. Even at the cellular level, their body was doing its best, operating with whatever nutritional resources it had. And so their death, as the combined effect of countless moments of Relative Peak Intelligence, could not have happened another way.

The same is true for someone who took his or her own life. After my half brother died, I had the thought that I could have done more. I had already been exploring a lot of self-help processes, and I remember trying a form of meditation before he died and thinking that it might help him (he had struggled with depression his whole life). But I didn't want to be pushy. Couldn't I have done more? In reality, no. *I didn't want to be pushy.* And obviously, I didn't know he would take his life.

Looking back at his death now through the lens of Relative Peak Intelligence, I can see that, given where the rest of us were mentally and emotionally, we were all doing our best. And looking at him, I can see that he was doing his best as well. I can see that his decision was an act of intelligence *in his eyes,* the highest act of intelligence he was capable of at that time. *That doesn't excuse us from creating better resources and reaching out to depressed people more effectively.* The future hasn't been written yet. But the past has, and seeing this clearly helps us focus our attention forward, not backward, so we can reach out to others more quickly.

In the case of someone who died by injury, Relative Peak Intelligence works a little differently. To help demonstrate this, I'll use the example of my little half sister.

She had been riding on the highway in the backseat of my stepmother's car when a truck driver in the next lane swerved to avoid someone in front of him. The truck jackknifed and toppled on the side of the car my sister was in. Someone might say that it could have happened another way—the truck driver could have not swerved, or the driver in front of him could have not cut in, or my sister could have been sitting somewhere else. In fact, people said all of these things. But none of them is true.

These statements are not true because the truck driver wasn't thinking, "If I turn the wheel this much I will avoid toppling on the car next to me, but I'm going to turn it more and flip over." He just did what he did, to the best of his ability. And the driver of the car in front of him didn't say, "I'm going to cut in front of this truck and cause a fatal accident." Maybe he had spilled coffee, or dropped something, or just had a lapse of attention and drifted into the next lane. I've done all of these things while driving and was fortunate not to have a truck in the lane next to me. But whatever happened, that driver was doing his best at that moment. Nowhere on that road that day will you find someone who wasn't doing his or her relative best.

And that's true for everything that has ever happened. No matter how unfortunate it turned out, no matter how avoidable it seemed later, when you look closer you'll see that everyone was doing the best they could at that time. They could not have chosen differently given their experience up to that point. This is why *there is nothing that ever took place that could have happened differently than it did.* What takes place is the sum total of everyone's best efforts. These efforts can be improved *in the future* as society evolves. But telling yourself that what already happened could have happened differently is an exercise not just in futility and denial but in real pain. And the way out of that pain is to fully see for yourself why this belief isn't true.

So look at the circumstances involved in the death of your loved one, and instead of seeing the avoidability of it, look for the *unavoidability* given the conditions in place. Look for the fact that no one really knew what would happen. Look for the fact that everyone was doing the best they could at the time (including you). And, since this book may fall into the hands of people struggling with events like those that took place at Fort Hood, Virginia Tech, and Columbine, look for the fact that mental imbalance is still part of the human experience and that sometimes this imbalance intersects violently with innocent lives. Breathe as you reflect on this, and take your time.

When you can see that, in reality, given the countless parts in motion, each doing their best, what took place could not have happened another way at that time, write it on your worksheet. Remind yourself that it doesn't let anyone off the hook. There may still be lawsuits and prison sentences. That doesn't have to change. But the more clearly you see Relative Peak Intelligence at work at all times, the more you stop fighting the past and thinking that it somehow got itself wrong. And this, then, may open you up to one final suggestion regarding the nature of death, given below.

In reality, they should have died at that time because death is not a punishment or a tragedy or even something "bad." Death is simply an expression of the same dynamics that produce life, dynamics beyond our ability to predict or control.

For this last proof, I'd like you to close your eyes and imagine a thousand dominoes lined up so that tipping one over will take them all down. Then imagine that the first 999 dominoes are in the dark, and you can see only the last one. When that last domino eventually topples over, someone might be shocked and say, "It shouldn't have fallen." But they can say this only if they aren't aware of all the other pieces in the chain.

Death is the end result of combined forces that we can't even begin to count. These forces come together to produce life, to sustain life, and then to end life. And when it comes to the end, whether or not we understand why, the last domino will fall. As long as you see this as a separate and tragic mistake, you live with a fearful and heavy heart. But what if death is not a tragedy or a mistake? What if death is part of the game of life, and not a violation of that game?

That doesn't mean that we *prefer* death. Life is beautiful. But it's possible to have a sense of ease in thinking about death. Seeing life and death as partners instead of as opponents removes the sadness, guilt, and regret that prevent you from fully engaging your memories of those you loved and continue to love. And it helps you enjoy your time now more fully.

If this makes sense to you, read over the suggested proof above, take a moment to think about it, and add it to your list. Breathe.

Now, read your list to yourself out loud. This is a big topic, and it's worth spending some time reflecting on. See if you can add any other proof. Here's what we have so far, in addition to whatever you came up with on your own.

5 Write below all the proof you can find that supports the negation being true in reality at this time (or in the past). Don't rush. Be thorough, using an additional sheet of paper if necessary.

> In reality, they should have died at that time because they were not immortal.

> In reality, they should have died at that time because the human body is fragile.

> In reality, they should have died at that time because our medical knowledge is still very limited.

> In reality, they should have died at that time because their body reached a definite point beyond which it could not sustain life.

> In reality, they should have died at that time because life makes no promises.

> In reality, they should have died at that time because it could not have happened another way.

> In reality, they should have died at that time because death is not a punishment or a tragedy or even something "bad." Death is simply an expression of the same dynamics that produce life, dynamics beyond our ability to predict or control.

Reading this list to yourself, can you begin to see that it's possible to realize that, in reality, someone *should* have died at that time, but not to mean that you wanted him or her to die? When you use "should" this way, you point it back to the real world. The cost of pointing it *away* from the real world is your own health and happiness. You may not feel particularly happy saying that in reality they should have died at that time, but you will feel less unhappy, because your fight with the world around you begins to end.

For me, this insight brought peace. Take time to see what feelings come with your own insights. There's no hurry. When you feel ready, fill out Step 6a.

6a How do you *feel* when you see the truth of the negation? (Circle below or add your own.)

calm   clear   compassionate   connected   curious

enlightened   enthusiastic   excited   free   grateful

honest   humble   intimate   light   loving   optimistic

peaceful   playful   relaxed   relieved   serene

supportive   tolerant   truthful   understanding

A change in how you think and feel always leads to a change in how you act. When I believed they shouldn't have died, I stopped studying, I became paranoid, I pitied myself, and I looked down on some of my friends as naïve. But when I saw that in reality they should have died at that time, all of this changed. Instead of seeing their lives as cut short or ruined by death, I could see their lives as whole, and I could be grateful for the time we had together. I also appreciated my own life more and the lives of people I loved who were still alive. All of that would go on my worksheet.

Think about how your actions could be different, then fill that out in 6b. If you're not feeling even a little bit of any of these feelings, you may want to go back to Step 5 and spend more time reflecting on the negation.

6b What *actions* might come from this?
(Circle below or add your own.)

accept   apologize   approach   be honest   breathe

clarify   communicate   contribute   delegate   exercise

explore   focus   follow through   forgive   give thanks

listen   make amends   network   open up   participate

prioritize   reach out   share   speak up   support

Finally, looking over your worksheet, how would you now rate the belief "They shouldn't have died"? In reality, how true is that? For me, fully taking in the truth of how their lives unfolded, that statement just isn't true. It's a 0. But take a few deep breaths and see what you come up with.

7 Read your original statement again. How strongly do you feel this belief to be true now?

0   1   2   3   4   5   6   7   8   9   10

weaker   ⟵————————

Congratulations on completing this worksheet. Even if you didn't drop any points, just making it all the way through this one is worth celebrating, because it's not easy to challenge deeply held beliefs.

If you did drop in points, and especially if you dropped more than five points, go for a walk, get some fresh air, and let yourself integrate some of what happened. You don't have to find yourself thinking anything specific. One of the strange things about a purely subtractive process like ActivInsight is that you can feel very different afterward, but have no idea why. It's as if something shifted that you can't put your finger on. This is because there's no new belief for your mind to cling to.

Instead of adding a new thought, such as "They're in heaven" or "Everything happens for a reason," what you did was challenge and subtract an old thought. You don't walk away saying, "They *should* have died," which could sound cold. Instead, you simply no longer carry the belief that they *shouldn't* have died (or don't carry it as strongly). This can open up a space inside your mind that is unfamiliar. But people who have done this worksheet have found that settling into that space is a peaceful experience, and that it profoundly changes both how they see their departed loved ones and how they live with what occurred.

This was the last worksheet we'll do together in this book. In the epilogue that follows, I want to talk about next steps, and where you can go from here.

EPILOGUE

Most people today believe deeply in the myth of stress. Every day, they complain about how stressful their lives are, pointing to their relationships, their bodies, and their jobs as proof.

They deal with this, naturally, by trying to eliminate the stress "out there." When this doesn't work, when the struggle to eliminate the stress "out there" becomes too exhausting, they either tell themselves that life is inherently stressful and resign themselves to permanent hardship, or they try Plan B: escape—drugs, music, movies, travel, shopping, exercise, and anything else they can find to distract themselves from the stressors making them so miserable.

When asked why they experience so much stress, they repeat the answer they've been told. "Humans," they say, "didn't evolve to handle so many stressors. Humans evolved to handle a single threat, such as a saber-toothed tiger, so that the fight-or-flight response kicked in for just a few frenzied minutes. But now it's as if saber-toothed tigers are attacking us all day long."

So what can be done about this?

"Nothing," they say. "I need to learn to relax more. That's the best I can do. Stress, after all, isn't going to go away. The stressors will always continue to exist. In fact," they say, "I should celebrate that, because it motivates me. Without stress in my life, I would sit around all day, stare at the moon, and drool."

All of this is not just fundamentally wrong. It's incredibly costly.

For individuals, the myth of stress costs you your health, your happiness, and your productivity as each unresolved issue takes its toll on your body, your mind, and your behaviors. For organizations, it costs people the clarity and focus they need to truly give their best effort and to sustain that effort in the face of ongoing change. Nationally and internationally, the costs may be even higher. We've become a planet of stressed-out people who blame one another for how we feel and then wonder why progress is so slow on issues we need to come together to solve.

This book is an attempt to change that.

In part 1, I explained how the myth of stress was born, why there are no stressors, and where stress really comes from—a certain kind of thinking made possible by a part of your brain that specializes in abstract thought. Other animals can think this way as well and also experience stress, but not to the degree and with the frequency that humans do. And one thing that other animals *can't* do is learn how to quickly challenge their thoughts to eliminate stress at its source.

In part 2, you learned how to do just that, as we applied ActivInsight together to a wide range of different issues: traffic, anger, conflict, money, success, regret, heartbreak, and more. Along the way, you learned about the ActivInsight SPIRAL, additive vs. subtractive processes, and Relative Peak Intelligence. And you read stories from other people who have used ActivInsight to experience insights and break through issues in their lives, like Dudley, who thought he shouldn't be at Phoenix House; Tom, who felt he needed to know what would happen to him; Lisa, who believed she shouldn't have married her husband; and Sabrina, who thought she wanted her boyfriend back; and many others.

If you did your part, their insights became your insights, and the person reading these words is not the same person who began this book. You may have already seen changes in your thinking, and in the way you respond to certain situations in your life. You probably also find yourself negating thoughts in your head over the course of the day, occasionally laughing at what you come up with. All of this is a very good start.

So where do you go from here?

First, I encourage you to make a commitment to not just talking about ActivInsight, and not just thinking about ActivInsight, but actually doing ActivInsight. Doing at least one worksheet a week takes only a few minutes, but it can change how you experience the entire week. It replaces your anger and frustration with greater understanding, spares your body the wear and tear of hormonal surges, and leaves your mind clear to make the best decisions you can. It's a powerful investment.

Some people "get" ActivInsight right away, and have no trouble doing worksheets on their own. Others, however, have difficulty figuring out how to phrase statements for Step 1, or find themselves unable to come up with much proof for the negation. It seems so easy when I coach you in the book, but it can seem maddeningly elusive when you're facing a blank worksheet on your own. I've seen this repeatedly over the last few years, and I have three solutions for you to consider.

First, organizing a group of friends to meet regularly and do worksheets together can help you commit to a schedule, and gives you the benefit of other people's suggestions when you're proving the negation. Other people often have an easier time seeing why our own beliefs are false than we do, and vice versa.

The second option is to find a cognitive therapist who appreciates the value of this process and is able to assist you in using it. I'm not a therapist, and this is a lay process designed to help people interested in helping themselves, but identifying beliefs and proving the negations are skills that good cognitive therapists do well. I've met several psychologists who are excited by this technique, and this can be a useful avenue for those who enjoy ActivInsight and also want live, in-person facilitation.

The third option is to work with me directly.

How? Think about how the Internet has changed the way you communicate, the way you work, and the way you shop. Now think about how it has changed the way you deal with problems in your life. For the most part it hasn't, simply because most transformational processes require in-person interaction. But ActivInsight doesn't. You've experienced this yourself as you worked through the issues in this book with me, even though I wasn't physically in the room with you. As long as I can make suggestions and you can reflect on them, we can work together without ever actually meeting physically. We're meeting in your thought process, where the change needs to occur.

The advantage to this approach is that it makes self-help far more scalable. A family, a church group, or an entire company could simultaneously challenge their beliefs step-by-step, and experience breakthroughs that change how they all handle difficult situations. The disadvantage, however, is that each person will have different issues to address, and the ones in this book may not be the ones you find most relevant to your life.

So here's my proposed solution. In *The Myth of Stress,* I gathered together a baker's dozen of commonly stressful topics, which you've now completed. At mythofstress.com, I am gathering together many more—related to addiction, cancer, divorce, relationships, student life, health and disease, leadership, politics, money, success, organizational development, religion, diversity, war, abuse, sex and sexuality, parenting, peer pressure, elder care, body image, activism, the environment, and much, much more. For each topic, you'll get step-by-step guidance from me just as you did here, where I formulate the statement for you, and gently coach you to consider proofs that you might not otherwise come up with. You can suggest new topics to explore, and even post your own. There are also interactive forums where you can ask questions, share your experiences, and help others deepen their insights into the challenges they are facing.

The online platform leverages the power of technology to make insight available to anyone at any time, and overcomes many of the hurdles that have prevented countless people from working on their issues: It's private. It's convenient. It's stigma-free. And it's inexpensive. This is the first mainstream tool that can deliver genuine resilience training to countless people at once. And paired with this book, it's the beginning of what I hope will become an insight revolution, where millions of people take responsibility for their mental and emotional states, transform their stress at its source, and live happier lives. This revolution doesn't require clandestine meetings or marches in the street. The only thing needed is more people having more insights. And it begins with you, and those you share this book with.

To light a spark, I've posted some information at mythofstress .com that can help you spread the word. If you have questions about ActivInsight, you can ask them there as well. (I've answered some of the most common ones in appendix 1.) And if you've had positive experiences doing ActivInsight in this book, or notice changes in your life taking place, I'd love to hear from you.

Sincerely,

Andrew Bernstein

mythofstress.com

ACKNOWLEDGMENTS

I'd like to acknowledge the people who made this book possible.

To the thousands of people I've taught ActivInsight to in living rooms, classrooms, conference rooms, and boardrooms: Thank you for your open-mindedness, your honesty, and your insights. Teaching is a two-way street, and this book couldn't have happened without you. An extra-special thank-you to those of you whose stories are featured here.

To Byron Katie: If I am ActivInsight's father, you are its grandmother. I'm proud of the family resemblance, and I am deeply grateful for the wisdom, clarity, and love you've shared with me over the years.

To Leslie Meredith, my editor at Free Press: I had suspected when we first met that you would be the best editor I could ask for. Now I know it.

To my agent, David Black: Thank you for being so good at what you do. I'm honored to have you on my team. Also at David Black Inc., a big thank-you to Linda Loewenthal, Susan Raihofer, Gary Morris, Antonella Iannarino, and Leigh Ann Eliseo. Thank you, Margot Schupf, for introducing me to David.

To the many people behind the scenes at Simon & Schuster who contributed in numerous ways to make this book happen: Martha Levin, Jill Siegel, Dominick Anfuso, Suzanne Donohue, Carisa Hays, Laura Cooke, Nicole Kalian, Caitlin Hayes, Donna Lof-

ACKNOWLEDGMENTS

fredo, Kathryn Higuchi, Eric Fuentecilla, Ela Schwartz Hnizdo, and Erich Hobbing. I'm grateful for your help along the way.

To my parents, my brothers, and my friends: Thank you for your support, your feedback, your companionship, and your love. I couldn't have done it without you.

And, finally, to Whitney: you're the best.

FREQUENTLY ASKED
QUESTIONS

Q: How do I integrate ActivInsight into my life?

A: In my experience, the best way to do this is to start by under-standing the theory behind it (part 1), and then apply it to a range of issues (part 2). You've just done that. The next step is to continue applying it to whatever you experience as stressful. Over the course of your week, identify the thoughts behind any negative emotional experiences, and make some time to work on these. Most of us are troubled by the same issues over and over, so finding these beliefs and challenging them pays off. Even doing just one worksheet a week—say, every Sunday— can make a big difference. You can do these on your own, with a therapist or a group of friends, or online at mythofstress.com.

Q: Do people generally have to do the same worksheet over and over, or does doing it once mean I don't have to do it again? How long does the insight typically stick?

A: It really depends on how clearly you see the belief as untrue. For example, if you work on "They shouldn't get so angry" and you end up at a 1, you'll never respond to anger the same way again. So it becomes a lifelong change. Anger still happens around you, but you see it the way you would see fire or rain, and you act accordingly. If you ended at a 6 on that worksheet, however, anger would still provoke certain thoughts and emotions in you. Initially, people may repeat worksheets because they're still learning to focus on Step 5, but when they get it and drop to under a 3 in Step 7, a shift takes place and the insight seems to last longer. I can't say whether or not it's permanent, but I know people from my very first workshops in 2004 who are still 0's on beliefs that were 10's for them, and they experience no stress in those situations. If that were to change, however, they would just go through another worksheet and bring their minds back to the real world.

Q: *Eventually, do you just do this in your head and not need to work on paper?*

A: Most people find themselves negating statements in their heads shortly after learning ActivInsight. This can deflate stress in the moment (and lead to some good laughs). For larger issues, though, and for any negative thoughts or emotions that linger, get out a worksheet and go through all seven steps. The act of writing and including the other steps helps you go deeper. Once you've had a real "Aha," you won't find yourself needing to negate the statement in your head. The issue simply won't arise for you as a problem. So what changes as you do more ActivInsight isn't that you eventually do it in your head, but that you don't need to do it at all. When stress does arise, though, you get out a worksheet.

Q: *Is there anything this doesn't work on? Aren't some situations so extreme that they have to be stressful?*

A: No experience is inherently stressful. If you are open-minded and know how to phrase Step 1 and find proof in Step 5, you can successfully apply ActivInsight to anything.

Q: I found your suggestions in Step 5 really helpful. When I do Activ-Insight on my own, I'm not able to come up with as much proof. Why is this? And is there a way around this?

A: We all have different skills. Some people are good at math or crossword puzzles. Some people happen to be good at coming up with proof for the negations. With ActivInsight, it is not essential for you personally to be skilled at coming up with proof in Step 5. If someone else can give you good suggestions to consider, you can reflect on those and make them your own insights, having just as deep an experience as if you had come up with the suggestions yourself. There are several ways to do this. You can form a *Myth of Stress* book club with others and do worksheets in a group. If one or more people in the group are good at coming up with proof, the whole group benefits. You can also find a therapist who uses ActivInsight and do worksheets with his or her facilitation. Cognitive therapy in particular and ActivInsight work well together, and several therapists have told me they use this with their clients.

A third option is to do ActivInsight with me online at mythofstress.com. There you'll find an e-learning platform where I coach you through topics just as I've done in the book. You choose the topic you want to work on, and I guide you step-by-step through an online worksheet. The advantage to doing it online is that there are many more topics than you have in the book. You can also ask questions and share experiences in the forums. More information is available at mythofstress.com.

Q: Isn't sadness a natural and normal part of the human experience? And isn't it healthy to experience sadness (or other negative emotions) when someone dies, or something else really hurtful happens?

A: This process is for the times when you don't want to be sad, even if it's considered normal or healthy. Finding the thoughts that produce these feelings and challenging them can help you return to peace of mind more quickly. But there are no "hurtful" things in the world. There are just things. The hurt is produced through your mind as a function of contracted beliefs.

Q: Can children do ActivInsight?

A: Yes. I've shared this with people as young as twelve. A friend of mine (a child psychologist) introduced this to her eight-year-old daughter. I'm working on a modified version of the worksheet for kids that gives them room to draw and express themselves a little more creatively.

Q: What do you do when everything seems to be going wrong in your life, and there's no single thought bothering you? How do I apply ActivInsight to my entire life?

A: Get a blank sheet of paper and write down all the thoughts swimming in your head—about your job, your kids, your partner, your money. As Albert Ellis might have said, get all the "should" out of your head, but put it on paper. Even a thought such as "Everything is going wrong in my life" would be worth including. Then go back over your list and put stars next to the three with the biggest charges, and work on those three. After doing these, you'll feel differently about your life. Then pick additional topics from your list until you're done or you don't feel stressed-out anymore.

Q: But are all these worksheets necessary? Couldn't I just exercise or learn to meditate and get rid of all the stress at once?

A: Yes and no. You would get rid of the awareness of stress, but the underlying beliefs would still be there, so the stress will eventually return. That's why I call these processes additive. With a subtractive approach, you identify the specific counterfactual thoughts that you contract around and have insights into these so that stress is no longer produced. People who turn to additive approaches to relieve their stress will have to repeat them indefinitely. Do ActivInsight for a period of time, though, and you'll find that stress becomes increasingly rare.

Q: *Do I need to attack my stressful thoughts whenever they come up?*

A: Some people have framed working with the mind in terms of a battle between you and your thoughts, but I don't see it this way. To me it's a process of education. When you experience stress, you're believing something that's not true. With ActivInsight, you test your belief and educate your mind so that you can see where you were mistaken. Believing that the mind is something you need to fight or attack only adds more stress. Seeing it in the context of education means that there's simply something you haven't yet learned. ActivInsight helps you learn it.

Q: *What can I do about anxiety, like when I go on job interviews or get sick and think the doctor is going to tell me it's something serious?*

A: Find the thought that is triggering the emotions. "I know I'm not going to get the job" or "I know this is something serious" could both be worth considering. When you no longer think that you know what you don't, the anxiety will diminish. Anxiety is always a function of false certainty.

Q: *What about repeated situations, like a parent who continually tells you you're worthless, or endless projects at work? How is it possible to eliminate stress from these ongoing situations?*

A: You don't experience repeated or ongoing situations. You experience the situation *now*. When this situation now is no longer stressful, it's no longer stressful. If the stress arises again, you can question your thoughts again. But it all happens in the moment, not over the course of time. Do a worksheet on your parents or your workload (e.g., "They shouldn't tell me I'm worthless," "I can't handle the workload") and help yourself see the situation more clearly. Then you may want to have a conversation with your parents or your boss about what's taking place, or you may have other ideas for ways to change things. But have an insight first, *then* take action. The situation may continue, but the sense that you have a problem doesn't have to. You can't get there by thinking about it, though. You have to actually go through the process of challenging the contracted thoughts step-by-step.

Q: *I want to teach ActivInsight to other people I know who are stressed out. How do I do that?*

A: Doing ActivInsight with someone else isn't as easy as it looks and requires learning a few skills with supervision. At this point in time, the book and mythofstress.com are the best ways to share this.

Q: *I tried describing my experience with ActivInsight to a friend, and found it really difficult. Any suggestions?*

A: I usually say the following: "Stress doesn't come from what's going on in your life—it comes from *your thoughts about* what's going on in your life. ActivInsight is a simple technique that transforms your thought process so that the stress is eliminated at its source." You can also refer them to my website that has good introductory material.

Q: *You say that there's no such thing as a stressor, but what if someone is injected with poison? That doesn't have to do with their thoughts. Wouldn't that be a legitimate stressor?*

A: I distinguish between psychological stress and physiological stress. I prefer to categorize the latter as part of homeostasis, or as some people prefer now, allostasis. So there may be some allostatic challenges, like poisons, that all humans experience as lethal. But if another animal does not experience that substance as lethal (if it has enzymes that can break it down, for example), then is it really a stressor, or even a poison? Everything is relative. For humans, there are substances that most of us would find physically challenging. I would call these stimuli, and reserve the concept of stress for psychological issues. But there are no stressors.

Q: *The worksheet doesn't list positive feelings and behaviors in Step 3, or negative feelings and behaviors in Step 6. Doesn't doing this bias the worksheet so that it looks like we're changing, when really we're just leaving these other parts out?*

A: We work on only stressful thoughts, so when you write down a stressful thought and then ask yourself how you feel in Step 3a, the answers should be stress related. If you also feel some positive feelings or take positive actions based on that thought, that's okay, but it's not the majority of what you feel or do or else that thought wouldn't be problematic. Similarly, when you have an insight and your thoughts shift, the feelings and resulting behaviors would shift as well. So the worksheet is designed around this natural movement. It doesn't determine the movement so much as reflect it, like a mirror, so you can see it more easily.

Q: *What about sexual abuse, rape, terminal illness, or the murder of a loved one? These aren't just thoughts that can be shifted through insight. They're terrible experiences that someone can never fully get over. Isn't it disrespectful and a little delusional to suggest that working on their thoughts can help people with this?*

A: Before I address the question of whether or not there are certain topics that are beyond the reach of ActivInsight, I want to point out something more important. This process requires an open door. If someone is not interested in looking at how their own thought process might be playing a part in the emotions that they feel, then there's nothing more to be said. When the door is locked, ActivInsight can't do anything for someone, because it doesn't "do" anything on its own. It's just a series of steps for someone to use.

When someone *is* interested, however, the door is open. Then that person (not someone else) has the power to see for herself if this approach can work on her issues. She can't know this hypothetically. The energy of her own open mind is essential. I can tell you that other people have done ActivInsight worksheets on the issues you named, as well as on other big issues, and found something surprisingly different from what you might imagine. But it has to start with people's willingness to look closely at their own convictions.

Q: *What about constant physical pain? How do I work on that?*

A: Studies have shown that when you address the cognitive component of pain—the thoughts like "I shouldn't be in so much pain," "I can't handle the pain," etc.—the *physical* experience becomes less painful. So doing worksheets like these can be really helpful. Pain can be hard to withstand, but stress on top of pain makes it much harder.

Q: *Is this process about learning to accept things as they are?*

A: Acceptance as traditionally taught is really a form of tolerance. True acceptance is something else. Instead of trying to accept life as it is, what this process does is help you stop believing painfully in life as it isn't. As a result, a kind of acceptance takes place, but it's a deep acceptance, the kind that comes not from effort but from giving up. *You* can't give up, though. You see that what you believed to be true is actually not true, and the giving up happens on its own. But this isn't what people would normally call acceptance. If I were to say to you, do you accept the fact that your heart is beating, you would probably think that question very strange. It's just true. You don't feel like you have to accept it. But that's real acceptance. It just is.

Q: Do you personally ever experience stress anymore?

A: Stress works the same for me as it does for anyone else. The only difference is that I've done a lot of worksheets, so it has become rare that I get stressed-out. But when I do, I get out a worksheet and go through all seven steps. Once you know how to do this well, you'll find yourself having deep insights quickly, and there will be very little that upsets or angers you. Situations still arise, but you handle them quickly and intelligently. Anyone can do this. All it takes is insight.

If you have a question that you would like to ask,
please visit mythofstress.com.

THE ACTIVINSIGHT
WORKSHEET

ActivInsight

1 Write a concise, complete sentence describing something that you experience as stressful. It's helpful to use the words "should" or "shouldn't." (Example: "They should listen to me.")

\>
_____

_____

2 How strongly do you feel this belief to be true?

0   1   2   3   4   5   6   7   8   9   10

————————————————————————————————⟶ *stronger*

3a How do you *feel* when you believe this? (Circle below or add your own.)

3b How do you *act* when you feel this way? (Circle below or add your own.)

afraid   abandoned   angry   annoyed
anxious   confused   depressed
desperate   embarrassed   frustrated
helpless   hopeless   hurt   impatient
inadequate   insecure   invisible
jealous   nervous   rejected
resentful   tense   upset   worried

argue   belittle   blame   bully   complain
cry   drink   eat   escape   fight
find fault with   give up   gossip   insult
interrupt   lose sleep   manipulate
obsess   overwork   pity myself   preach
pretend   procrastinate   shop   shut down
smoke   suffer   withdraw   yell

4 Write the negation of your statement from Step 1. In most cases, you also add "In reality" at the beginning and "at this time" or "at that time" at the end.

\>
_____

_____

Continue to Step 5 . . .

5 Write below all the proof you can find that supports the negation being true in reality at this time (or in the past). Don't rush. Be thorough, using an additional sheet of paper if necessary.

> _____

> _____

> _____

> _____

> _____

> _____

Read what you found out loud to yourself. Can you come up with any more proof? Do you see the negation as true in reality?

 6a How do you *feel* when you see the truth of the negation? (Circle below or add your own.)

calm   clear   compassionate   connected
curious   enlightened   enthusiastic
excited   free   grateful   honest
humble   intimate   light   loving
optimistic   peaceful   playful   relaxed
relieved   serene   supportive   tolerant
truthful   understanding

 6b What *actions* might come from this? (Circle below or add your own.)

accept   apologize   approach   be honest
breathe   clarify   communicate
contribute   delegate   exercise   explore
focus   follow through   forgive
give thanks   listen   make amends
network   open up   participate   prioritize
reach out   share   speak up   support

 7 Read your original statement from Step 1 again. How strongly do you feel this belief to be true now?

0   1   2   3   4   5   6   7   8   9   10

weaker ⟵ _____

Congratulations, you've completed your ActivInsight worksheet. Review it later in the day to deepen your insights further. © ActivInsight, Inc.   All rights reserved.